101

Great Answers to the Toughest Interview Questions

By Ron Fry

THE CAREER PRESS
180 FIFTH AVE.,
PO BOX 34
HAWTHORNE, NJ 07507
1-800-CAREER-1
201-427-0229 (OUTSIDE U.S.)
FAX: 201-427-2037

**101 GREAT ANSWERS TO THE TOUGHEST
INTERVIEW QUESTIONS**
ISBN 1-56414-017-2, $7.95

Cover design by Harvey Kraft

Copies of this book may be ordered by mail or phone directly from the publisher. To order by mail, please include price as noted above, $2.50 handling per order, plus $1.00 for each book ordered. (New Jersey residents please add 7% sales tax.) Send to: The Career Press Inc., 180 Fifth Avenue., PO Box 34, Hawthorne, NJ 07507.

Or call Toll-Free 1-800-CAREER-1 to order using your VISA or Mastercard or for further information on all titles published or distributed by Career Press.

Attention: Schools, Organizations, Corporations

This book is available at quantity discounts for bulk purchases for educational, business or sales promotional use.
Please contact: Ms. Gretchen Fry,
Career Press,
180 Fifth Ave.,
Hawthorne, NJ 07507
or call 1-800-CAREER-1

Contents

The Interrogation

I still break out in a cold sweat when I remember *my* first job interview.

I had stayed up all night, pouring over the syllabus of every course I had taken since junior high school, ready to discuss how *each and every one of them* had served, amazingly enough, only to prepare me for the job I was trying to land.

In front of my favorite rehearsal mirror, I had waxed poetic about the awesome responsibilities the local grocery store had placed on me, its part-time summer worker.

And I had memorized ten show-stopping questions about my prospective employer's business, whose bottom line I knew better than my checking account.

By God, I was ready for Mr. Hogan, the man who, I imagined, would one day be thanking his lucky stars that he had found the very best proofreader in Creation—*me!*

When the round-shouldered, tweed-jacketed Mr. Hogan came out to the reception area to greet me, my confidence rose four notches. Why, he looked like a pushover! A Mr. Peeperish nebbish I could have my way with. In no time at all, I thought smugly, I wouldn't have to worry about lowly proofreading at all. By gum, I would have Hogan's job!

I sat down across from Mr. Hogan. He studied his desk for a split second, looked up at me, and said, "So, tell me about yourself."

Suddenly I could feel my nerve endings stand on end. And I swear I could *hear* my brain giving my palms the signal to sweat...profusely. Never before had I realized the full meaning of the word "swoon."

While I smiled and desperately reconfigured some of the little speeches I had been so diligently rehearsing for days, my reply still sputtered forth, filled with an embarrassing number of "ahs" and "ums."

I didn't get that job, let alone Mr. Hogan's! And I've often wondered if the fact that I couldn't be more convincing and confident when I was trying to tell him "a little bit about myself" was the reason.

Scrapbook of Golden Memories

My next few interviews weren't much better. But, thanks to a level of impatience with *any* employment situation that would give any career counselor pause, I've gone on a *lot* of job interviews. Like the piano, practice makes perfect—I got better at them. I think there was a time in my life when I even started anticipating job interviews with some sort of perverted enthusiasm.

This book is intended to make your memories of interviews more like the ones I had later in life, rather than the bad dreams I still have about Grand Inquisitor Hogan. It will give you a preview of the questions you're most likely to face during an interview, help you prepare terrific answers for them, and, as a consequence, make you feel far more prepared, far more confident...and far more likely to get the job!

I've devoted entire chapters to the toughest questions—those open-ended ones such as, "Now, tell me a little about yourself"—and grouped others into chapters dealing with the most common *types* of interview questions. (Just to show I have titled this book accurately, I have numbered the questions in the book consecutively—that is, the first question in chapter 2 ["So, tell me about yourself," naturally] is "1," the last question [in chapter 12] is "101." And note that all 101 questions are listed in chapter 13, along with chapter and page references.)

This book is *not* designed, however, to turn you into some well-trained parrot who can reel off snappy answers to any question your prospective employers can muster. Instead, it is a manual that will help you understand something about interviewing techniques, and what it is—*exactly*—that the interviewer is trying to get at...with each and every question he or she asks.

While this book provides a host of good answers to common interview questions, the very best replies will come from you. After all, you're in the best position to know how to let your genuine talents shine through during the very artificial situation of an employment interview. So use my answers as a starting point, "hints," if you will, on how to frame your own great answers.

In addition, this book is intended to arm you with knowledge—the key to mastering what could be your greatest enemies during the interviewing process: fear and anxiety.

How to Use This Book

After reading the first two chapters, which discuss the interview process in a general way, begin writing down *your* answers to the questions presented in the following chapters, using the sample answers *as guidelines.*

Refine these answers and read them over and over again so you become familiar and comfortable with them. You *should* take the time to memorize some of your answers—don't worry, I'll tell you which ones—so that you can repeat them *verbatim* to the interviewer, but in a way that sounds spontaneous and enthusiastic, not tired and rehearsed.

This might sound like a daunting challenge right now. But I assure you, by the time you finish this book, you'll actually be looking forward to the challenge of job interviews. And you'll be *good* at them!

So, good luck. And try to keep those palms dry!

Chapter 1

No, You Can't
Just Wing It

Quick! Think of a salesperson you've encountered who really *sold* you. Not someone who used such high-pressure tactics that you said "yes" just so he'd shut up, but a salesperson to whom you'd actually send your best friend, convinced you'd be doing her a favor.

What was it about that person that made you want to buy from him? Almost certainly it was the person's *knowledge* of his product—the comfortable way in which he could talk about that car, the refrigerator, or the lawn furniture that convinced you to pry your credit card out of your wallet and *buy what he was selling.*

The Product is *You*

Realizing that knowledge of his or her product is what characterizes a good *professional* salesperson makes it all the more astounding that most candidates show up for job interviews insufficiently prepared to talk about the most important thing *they* will ever have to sell—themselves.

In answer to many typical job-interview questions, most candidates will hesitate, then stump and stutter their way through a disjointed litany of resume fragments. Or recite some obviously "canned" reply that shows the trained interviewer only that the candidate has developed memorization skills good enough to be a tour guide.

The sad fact is that most job candidates are unprepared to talk about themselves. Sure, they might be wearing the perfect clothes and have prepared gorgeous resumes, but they are still poorly armed for this important sell *if that's all they've got in their arsenal.*

The object of this chapter is to get you ready for one—that's right, one and *only one*—question: **Who are you?** Because every *other* question the interviewer asks you will be geared to finding a few more pieces to the puzzle of "Who are you?"—the mother of all interview questions.

To come up with the best answer, you will have to sit down and compose a brief history of your life.

What You Should Know About You

Your first step in becoming a *successful* job candidate—and not just another foot-sore veteran of the unemployment line—is to build a dossier about yourself, one you'll review until you are entirely familiar with its every detail. It will help you develop credible, convincing answers to typical interview questions, answers that will set you apart from the herd.

I've given you eight important *Data Input Sheets* at the end of this chapter to help you organize this information about yourself.

Here's the information to put on each one.

Employment Data Input Sheet

First, assemble information on every full- and part-time job you've ever held. Include:

- Each employer's name, address, and telephone number
- The names of all of your supervisors and, whenever possible, where they can be reached
- Exact dates you were employed at each company
- The dates you received promotions
- In the case of part-time jobs, the number of hours worked per week
- Specific duties and responsibilities
- The number of people you supervised
- Financial responsibilities/purchasing authority
- Specific skills utilized
- Key accomplishments
- Honors and special recognition
- Copies of awards, letters of recommendation

Pay particular attention to recording information that will demonstrate the important qualities that employers are looking for in successful job candidates. Don't write until you think your hand will fall off, but *do* write *all* of the data that you will try to get across during your interview:

Duties—Write one or two sentences describing what you did in each of the jobs you held. Use numbers as much as possible to provide some objective measurement to the scope of these duties. For instance, an experienced salesperson might write: "Responsible for management of 120 active accounts in sales territory that contributed $3 million in annual revenues. Reviewed activity of three telephone-sales personnel."

Skills—Enumerate the specific capabilities required to perform the job or those that you developed while you were in the job. Here is where you should establish your bragging rights. If you achieved specific results, write them down.

Some examples: "Developed new call-reporting system," "Increased volume in territory 20% within 18 months," "Oversaw computerization of department that helped realize cost savings of 15%."

Prepare an employment data sheet for each job you've held, *no matter how short the tenure or how limited you may think it is.* Yes, even summer jobs are important here, since they demonstrate resourcefulness, industriousness, and the fact that you had a sense of independence and responsibility even when you were living at home.

Volunteer Work Data Input Sheet

Having hired more than 100 people during my career, I can attest to the fact that your "after-hours" activities can mean a lot to employers. I've been very impressed by candidates' references to books they've read, activities they enjoy, information that gives me a sense of their *values.* After all, selfish or limited people are rarely the best employees.

Therefore, don't dismiss from careful consideration activities for which you don't get a paycheck when you're performing these exercises. After all, we're not after the "9-to-5" you, but the *real* you. Keep the same detailed notes on volunteer activities as you have on jobs you've held:

- Each organization's name, address and telephone number
- Name of supervisor or director of the organization
- Exact dates you began (and ended) involvement with the organization
- Approximate number of hours devoted to the activity monthly
- Specific duties and responsibilities

- Specific skills utilized
- Accomplishments, honors
- Copies of awards, letters of recommendation

Educational Data Input Sheets

If you're a college graduate, omit details on high school. If still in college, omit all but the most sterling high school records.

If you're a graduate student, list details on both graduate and undergraduate coursework. If you have not yet graduated, list your anticipated date of graduation. If more than a year away, indicate the numbers of credits earned through the most recent semester to be completed.

Activities Data Input Sheet

List all sports, clubs or other activities in which you've participated, either inside or outside school. For each you should include:

- Name of activity/club/group
- Offices held
- Purpose of club/activity
- Specific duties/responsibilities
- Achievements, accomplishments, awards

Awards and Honors Data Input Sheet

List awards and honors from your school(s) (prestigious high school awards can still be included here, even if you're in graduate school or long out of school), community groups, church groups, clubs, etc.

Military Service Data Input Sheet

Complete military history, if pertinent, including:

- Dates of service
- Final rank awarded
- Duties and responsibilities
- All citations and awards
- Details on specific training and/or any special schooling
- Skills developed
- Specific accomplishments

Many useful skills are learned in the armed forces, besides, of course, disarming nuclear weapons. As the commercials say, a tour in the military often speeds up the maturation process, making you a more attractive candidate. So, if you have served in the armed forces, make sure you have the details ready to discuss.

Language Data Input Sheet

This can be a very important section for those of you with a real proficiency in a second language. And *do* make sure you have at least conversational fluency in the language(s) you list. One year of college Russian doesn't count, but if you spent a year studying in Moscow, you are probably fluent or near fluent.

Such a talent could be invaluable, especially if you hope to work in the international arena (which is increasingly important for more and more U.S. companies).

Is That All There Is?

These forms now contain a great deal of information, but all they really reveal about you is what you've done and where you've been, or, as *Dragnet*'s Sergeant Friday might put it, "just the facts, ma'am, just the facts."

But there is a whole lot more to you than just the facts, and that is precisely what the trained interviewer will be looking for. The facts you've recorded on the data input sheets should provide a means to think about what makes you, YOU. Take a look at them and ask yourself questions like these:

1. Which of the achievements you enjoyed at work or in school make you the proudest? What bearing will these accomplishments have on your future career?

2. What failures in your life do you think about most often? Why did they occur? Have you done anything to keep similar things from occurring again? Have you learned from your mistakes? How?

3. How do you interact with authority figures—bosses, teachers, parents? Have these interactions demonstrated failure or success with authority figures?

These exercises will be most valuable if you write down your answers. Because this confessional writing will be for your eyes only, you don't have to be concerned about producing beautiful prose or even complete sentences. The only important thing—in fact, the *crucial* thing—is honesty.

You're in for a Big Surprise

If you've been brutally frank and honest, this exercise has probably told you things about yourself you never realized,

maybe some things you wish you didn't know. This type of
exercise is very difficult, but it's not over just yet. You have to
get to know yourself just a little better.

Get some fresh paper and start writing. Here are some
more tough questions:

1. What are your favorite games and sports? Think
   about the way you play these games and what that
   says about you. Are you overly competitive? Do you
   give up too easily? Are you a good loser or a bad
   winner? Do you rise to a challenge or back away
   from it?

2. What kinds of people do you generally make friends
   with? Do you look to associate only with people who
   are very similar to you? Do you enjoy or merely
   tolerate differences in others? What are the things
   that have caused you to end friendships? What does
   this say about you?

3. If you were to ask a group of friends and acquain-
   tances to describe you, what adjectives would they
   use? List *all* of them, the good and the bad. Why
   would people describe you in this way? Are there
   specific behaviors, skills, achievements, failures
   that lead to the use of these adjectives? What are
   they?

What's the Point?

You might be wondering by now, "Hey, what's the point of
all this soul searching? After all, I'm just trying to get ready
for a job interview."

Well, the point is that this self-examination will help you
develop a better description of the product you're selling—

you—when you meet your prospective employer. As you might have learned in a marketing class or during the course of your career, the best way to sell someone is to describe the *features* of a product and the *benefits* each of those features provides.

Looking over your data input sheets and the answers to the questions posed above, you should now develop several lists of your "features" under the following headings:

- Strongest skills
- Greatest areas of knowledge
- Strongest parts of my personality
- The things I do best
- Skills that I should develop to do better in my career
- Areas of my personality that I should improve

You will be amazed at the results of this exercise if you take the time to do it correctly—and if you're brutally honest with yourself. It should help you realize things about yourself that you never knew, or, more accurately, that you never *knew* that you knew.

Here's the Point

I urge you to do these exercises when there is no imminent need to use the information—that is, *now*, before you have your first job interview scheduled. Then, when you have your first interview set up, take out your lists and a clean sheet of paper and answer *these* questions:

1. What in my personal inventory will convince this employer that I deserve the position?

2. What are the strengths, achievements, skills, and areas of knowledge that make me most qualified for this position? What in my background should separate me from the applicant pack?

3. What weaknesses should I admit to, if asked about them, and how will I indicate that I will have improved them?

Is This Any Way to Prepare?

This is the *only* way to prepare to answer the questions that come up time and time again during employment interviews. Take your time with this exercise so that you will be able to discuss the most important product you'll ever have to sell—yourself.

If you're unconvinced that this series of exercises is *absolutely essential*, read on. I'm sure that the chapters ahead, filled with interviewer questions and suggestions about how to answer them, will absolutely convince you that conducting a personal inventory is the best way to assure that you will hit prospective employers with your best shot.

EMPLOYMENT DATA INPUT SHEET

Employer Name:_____

Address:_____

Address:_____

Phone:_____

Dates of Employment: _____ to _____

Hours Per Week: _____ Salary/Pay:_____

Supervisor's Name & Title: _____

Duties:_____

_____

_____

Skills Utilized:_____

_____

_____

Accomplishments/Honors/Awards: _____

_____

_____

Other Important Information:_____

_____

EMPLOYMENT DATA INPUT SHEET

Employer Name: _____

Address: _____

Address: _____

Phone: _____

Dates of Employment: _____ to _____

Hours Per Week: _____ Salary/Pay: _____

Supervisor's Name & Title: _____

Duties: _____

_____

_____

Skills Utilized: _____

_____

_____

Accomplishments/Honors/Awards: _____

_____

_____

Other Important Information: _____

_____

EMPLOYMENT DATA INPUT SHEET

Employer Name: _____

Address: _____

Address: _____

Phone: _____

Dates of Employment: _____ to _____

Hours Per Week: _____ Salary/Pay: _____

Supervisor's Name & Title: _____

Duties: _____

_____

_____

Skills Utilized: _____

_____

_____

Accomplishments/Honors/Awards: _____

_____

_____

Other Important Information: _____

_____

_____

EMPLOYMENT DATA INPUT SHEET

Employer Name: _____

Address: _____

Address: _____

Phone: _____

Dates of Employment: _____ to _____

Hours Per Week: _____   Salary/Pay: _____

Supervisor's Name & Title: _____

Duties: _____

_____

_____

Skills Utilized: _____

_____

_____

Accomplishments/Honors/Awards: _____

_____

_____

Other Important Information: _____

_____

_____

VOLUNTEER WORK DATA INPUT SHEET

Organization Name: _____

Address: _____

Address: _____

Phone: _____ Hours Per Week: _____

Dates of Activity: _____

Supervisor's Name & Title: _____

Duties: _____

_____

_____

Skills Utilized: _____

_____

_____

Accomplishments/Honors/Awards: _____

_____

_____

Other Important Information: _____

_____

_____

VOLUNTEER WORK DATA INPUT SHEET

Organization Name: _____

Address: _____

Address: _____

Phone: _____ Hours Per Week: _____

Dates of Activity: _____

Supervisor's Name & Title: _____

Duties: _____

_____

_____

Skills Utilized: _____

_____

_____

Accomplishments/Honors/Awards: _____

_____

_____

Other Important Information: _____

_____

_____

HIGH SCHOOL DATA INPUT SHEET

School Name: _____

Address: _____

Address: _____

Phone: _____ Years Attended: _____

Major Studies: _____

GPA/Class Rank: _____

Honors: _____

Important Courses: _____

OTHER SCHOOL DATA INPUT SHEET

School Name: _____

Address: _____

Address: _____

Phone: _____ Years Attended: _____

Major Studies: _____

GPA/Class Rank: _____

Honors: _____

Important Courses: _____

COLLEGE DATA INPUT SHEET

College:_____

Address:_____

Phone:_____   Years Attended:_____

Degrees Earned:_____   Major:_____

Minor:_____   Honors:_____

_____

Important Courses:_____

_____

_____

GRADUATE SCHOOL DATA INPUT SHEET

College:_____

Address:_____

Phone:_____   Years Attended:_____

Degrees Earned:_____   Major:_____

Minor:_____   Honors:_____

_____

Important Courses:_____

_____

ACTIVITIES DATA INPUT SHEET

Club/Activity: _____

Office(s) Held: _____

Description of Participation: _____

_____

Duties/Responsibilities: _____

_____

_____

Club/Activity: _____

Office(s) Held: _____

Description of Participation: _____

_____

Duties/Responsibilities: _____

_____

_____

Club/Activity: _____

Office(s) Held: _____

Description of Participation: _____

_____

Duties/Responsibilities: _____

_____

ACTIVITIES DATA INPUT SHEET

Club/Activity:_____

Office(s) Held:_____

Description of Participation:_____

_____

Duties/Responsibilities:_____

_____

_____

Club/Activity:_____

Office(s) Held:_____

Description of Participation:_____

_____

Duties/Responsibilities:_____

_____

_____

Club/Activity:_____

Office(s) Held:_____

Description of Participation:_____

_____

Duties/Responsibilities:_____

_____

AWARDS & HONORS DATA INPUT SHEET

Name of Award, Citation, Etc.: _____

From Whom Received: _____

Date: _____   Significance: _____

_____

Other Pertinent Information: _____

_____

_____

Name of Award, Citation, Etc.: _____

From Whom Received: _____

Date: _____   Significance: _____

_____

Other Pertinent Information: _____

_____

_____

Name of Award, Citation, Etc.: _____

From Whom Received: _____

Date: _____   Significance: _____

_____

Other Pertinent Information: _____

_____

MILITARY SERVICE DATA INPUT SHEET

Branch:_____

Rank (at Discharge):_____

Dates of Service:_____

Duties & Responsibilities:_____

_____

_____

_____

Special Training and/or School Attended:_____

_____

_____

_____

_____

Citations, Awards, etc.:_____

_____

_____

Specific Accomplishments:_____

_____

_____

_____

LANGUAGE DATA INPUT SHEET

Language:_____

☐ Read   ☐ Write   ☐ Converse

Background (number of years studied, travel, etc.): _____

_____

_____

_____

Language:_____

☐ Read   ☐ Write   ☐ Converse

Background (number of years studied, travel, etc.): _____

_____

_____

_____

Language:_____

☐ Read   ☐ Write   ☐ Converse

Background (number of years studied, travel, etc.): _____

_____

_____

_____

Chapter 2

The Killer Question

1. So, tell me a little about yourself!

I've always been an advocate of getting the most difficult things out of the way first. So in a book designed to help you prepare for job-interview questions, I feel compelled to deal with this, the absolute *favorite* question of all interviewers (okay, so it's not *really* a question!) and the *least* favorite of most candidates.

This little interrogatory puts you on the spot in a way no other question can. It turns up the spotlight *and* your pulse and makes your throat go dry...especially if you are unprepared for it.

However, if you *are* prepared, it gives you the opportunity to show interviewers the four traits they are looking for most in job candidates: enthusiasm, confidence, dependability, and intelligence.

Prepare to be Prepared

"So, tell me a little about yourself" is among the favorite icebreakers of seasoned interviewers (the type you'll usually meet in personnel departments) because it gives them a chance to study an encyclopedia of reactions, from verbal cues to candidates' body language.

It is also a favorite of *un*trained interviewers, such as hiring managers, simply because they don't know what else to ask. In fact, untrained interviewers are more likely to ask this question to fill "dead air," rather than as a means to get the interview off and running.

How to prepare? Well, developing a successful answer to this common question is one of the key reasons I urged you to complete a personal inventory in chapter 1. (If you haven't done so, please do before reading on.) Take a good look at it now, particularly those items under the headings:

- My strongest skills
- Greatest areas of knowledge
- Strongest parts of my personality
- Things I do best
- Key accomplishments

Speech! Speech!

Now, take the information under those headings and mold it into a speech of 250 to 350 words (roughly 60 to 90 seconds when spoken). What should this speech be like? Here is a generic outline:

1. Brief introduction to wonderful, wonderful *you*
2. Your key accomplishments
3. The key strengths demonstrated by these accomplishments
4. The importance of these strengths and accomplishments to your prospective employer

5. Where and how you see yourself developing in the position for which you're applying (just to add the right amount of modesty)

To give you a better idea of how these little speeches should read, let's look at a couple of examples.

Here is what a recent college graduate applying for an entry-level sales position might say:

> "I've always been able to get along with different types of people. I think it's because I'm a good talker and an even better listener. When I began thinking seriously about what careers I'd be best suited for, I thought of sales almost immediately.
>
> "That thought really stuck in my senior year of high school and during summers at college when I worked various part-time jobs at retail outlets because, unlike most of my friends, I actually *liked* dealing with the public.
>
> "However, I also realized that retail had its limitations. I read about various sales positions and was particularly fascinated by what is usually described as consultative selling. I like the idea of going to a client that you've really done your homework on and showing him how your products can help him solve one of his nagging problems and then following through on that.
>
> "I wrote one of the papers in my senior year on the subject of consultative selling, and that led me to begin looking for companies at which I could learn and refine the skills shared by people who've become more like account executives than run-of-the-mill salespeople.

"That led me to your company, Mr. Shannon. I find the prospect of working with companies to increase the energy efficiency of their installations an exciting one. I've also learned some things about your sales training programs, and they sound like they're on the cutting edge.

"I guess the only thing I find a little daunting about the prospect of working at Cogeneration, Inc. is selling that highly technical equipment without an engineering degree. By the way, what sort of support does your technical staff lend to the sales effort?"

Not a bad little speech, huh? This fine candidate—let's call her Barb—has:

1. *Introduced the requisite amount of modesty* before beginning to brag about herself ("I think it's because...").

2. *Laid claim to the single most important skill* a good, consultative salesperson should have (the ability to get along with others).

3. *Demonstrated industriousness* and at least some related experience (part-time positions in high school and college).

4. *Showed a decided interest* in the scope of the job (the term paper and the research on the company).

5. *Gave concrete evidence* of some of the other skills any good employee should have: the tendency to be a good self-starter (again, by mentioning the research on the company), a willingness to learn (reference to the training programs), and deference to authority (the question about technical support).

6. ***Provided herself a breather*** by ending with a question, one he'll have to take some time to answer.

That's quite a list of accomplishments for a mere 275-word speech, isn't it?

Let me give you another example before providing a list of pointers on how you can tailor-make a speech to fit *your* personal inventory.

Kenny has had nearly a decade of experience in his field. He is applying for his dream job, but he knows he has a couple of strikes against him—he's moved around a bit (four jobs) and doesn't quite have enough management experience.

He's applying for a job as a general manager of a district office for a firm providing maintenance services to commercial and residential properties. It is a demanding job, virtually the equivalent of running one's own $7-million per year business.

Kenny sweated out the preparation for his big chance, anticipated the potentially devastating interview punch ("Tell me something that will help me get a better feel for you than I get here on the resume."), and came up with the winning counterpunch:

> "I am a hard worker who loves this business. I've been an asset to the employers I've had, and my experience would make me an even greater asset to you.
>
> "I think these are the most exciting times that I've ever seen in this business. Sure, there's so much more competition now, and it's harder than ever to get really good help. But all the indications are that more and more companies will outsource their maintenance needs and that more two-income households will require the services that we provide.

"How do we get a bigger share of this business? How do we recruit and train the best personnel because they are, after all, the secret of our success? Those are the key challenges managers face in this industry.

"I can help your company meet those challenges. While resumes don't tell the whole story, mine demonstrates that: 1. I'm a hard worker. I've had promotions at every company I've worked for. 2. I would bring a good perspective to the position because I've been a doer, as well as a supervisor. People that work for me always respect my judgment, because they know I have a very good understanding of what *they* do. And 3. I have a terrific business sense. I'm great at controlling expenses. I deploy staff efficiently. I'm fair. And I have a knack for getting along with customers.

"I've always admired your company. I must admit I have adopted some of CleanShine's methods and applied them in the companies I've worked for.

"I see now that you're branching into lawn care. I was a landscaper during my high-school summers. How is that business going?"

Way to go, Kenny! In a mere 275 words, this successful general manager candidate managed to:

1. *Focus the interviewer* only on the positive aspects of his resume. Sure, Kenny has moved around a lot, but, after this answer, the interviewer might think, "Gee, look at all he's managed to accomplish everywhere he's gone."

2. *Get the interview started* the way *he* wanted it to go. He demonstrated experience, leadership capabilities, and a good understanding of the market.

3. *Introduce just the right amount of humility* into what is a fairly braggart-like answer to the question ("I must admit...").

   The result: Kenny has portrayed himself as a roll-up-the-shirtsleeves type of manager who will have trouble neither in getting along with blue-collar workers nor in discussing strategies with the "suits" back at headquarters.

4. *Turn things over to the interviewer* with a very informed question.

Note that both Barb and Kenny did *not* attempt to write and memorize an answer that would make a professional writer proud. Sentence structure is correct and gramatical, but it is not overly complicated. There is a sprinkling of industry "jargon" in Kenny's answer, but it is appropriate.

The more "perfect" you try to make the words in such an answer—replacing every word with its higher-falutin cousin from your thesaurus, making every paragraph a single, multiple-claused sentence—the more articifical it will sound.

Just make sure the five key points in the generic outline are covered—a brief introduction, key accomplishments, key strengths, the importance of them all and how you see yourself fitting in—and that you communicate the information you want to in a clear and concise manner.

Hey, Who's Running This Interview, Anyway?

One of the most important things to note in Kenny's reply is that he approached the interview knowing *what he wanted to accomplish* during it.

So many candidates go into the interview like cadavers being wheeled in for a med school anatomy class—they just sit there, letting the interviewer slice them apart. They spend far more time on wardrobe selection than answer preparation.

Kenny's answer should demonstrate how wrong-headed that approach can be.

It is essential for you to develop an *interview strategy* so your strengths can shine through and your weaknesses never surface (or, if they do, do so in a context that makes them seem relatively minor and unimportant). This strategy should help you determine how you will answer almost any of the questions put to you during the screening interview or the interview with the hiring manager.

Did You Do Your Homework?

I hope these first two chapters have convinced you of the importance of completing the personal inventory and going to the interview not *only* well dressed, but well *prepared.*

In the next chapter, we'll discuss how to establish an interview strategy and the two very different types of interviews you're likely to face.

But before you move ahead, review the key points to remember from this chapter.

Getting Ready for the Killer Question

- If you haven't already done so, fill out the personal inventory, as detailed in chapter 1.
- Distill your personal inventory into a compelling picture of *you* as the worker.
- Include in this verbal portrait words and phrases that convey enthusiasm, knowledge, confidence, intelligence, experience (if you have it!), eagerness to learn, and dependability. In the world of sports, these are usually summed up in the phrase "good attitude."
- In case this question is asked early in the interview, be sure that it helps set the course *you* want the interview to take. If you want to talk about your experience, play it up. Make the potential negatives (job-hopping, lack of experience, etc.) positive or irrelevant. (This, of course, might require the writing skills of Joseph Conrad, so work hard!)
- Write a 250- to 350-word reply. Rewrite it. Rewrite it again. Then rewrite it *again*. Get it to sound as conversational as possible, and practice saying it until it does.
- Memorize this speech and repeat it over and over until it sounds as though you never rehearsed it at all. Sounding like you're reading from internal cue cards during the interview will be a sure turnoff.
- Put the ball back in the interviewer's court by ending your little speech with a question. This will help give you a breather and, again, demonstrate enthusiasm.

Chapter 3

What You're Up Against

For employers, interviewing has made the transition from art to science.

A long-time subscriber to journals for human resources executives, I've lately seen myriad articles extolling the virtues of such things as "database interviews," "situational interviews," and "stress (confrontational) interviews."

While these techniques each have their own nuances, they have been developed with one goal in mind: to measure more accurately and reliably how a candidate will perform *on the job* if hired.

Personnel Petrie Dishes

Like scientists, interviewers are now expected to gather similar types of information on all the specimens they study—information that can be measured, quantified, and more easily and accurately compared. In fact, sometimes it seems as if *quantification* has replaced *qualification* in the hiring process.

The reasons are not as much Orwellian as economic. The "cost of hire"—the amount of money it takes to land a suitable candidate for a job—has escalated dramatically, and it will continue to increase as a result of the baby bust and the much ballyhooed shrinkage of the work force.

In addition, lawsuits against employers for wrongful discharge and other employment-related causes have increased exponentially over the past decade, making it more important for companies to hire people they (hope they) won't want to get rid of.

And, last but not least, for companies in our new Service Economy, the human resource is unquestionably the most valuable in their inventories.

Translation: Interviews Will be Tougher Than Ever

Not to make you more nervous about the prospect of job interviews than you probably already are, but interviewing is going to get harder and harder for job candidates at *all* levels of experience.

You probably will have to go through more interviews than your predecessors—whatever job you're after, whatever your level of expertise—as well as tests designed to measure your honesty, intelligence, mental health...and blood toxicity.

The good news is that most of the newest interviewing techniques are being practiced by personnel department staffers, usually the only ones who have the time to *read* about these new techniques.

Meanwhile, hiring managers, who barely have the time to do their jobs effectively, let alone stay current on the latest and greatest interviewing methods, are by-and-large using more traditional (i.e., "outdated") techniques. (Which, as we'll see later, can be both good news and bad news for you.)

The Screening Interview

If you are pursuing a job at a mid-size or large company (any organization of more than 250 employees), your first interview will often be with an employment or staffing manager in the personnel department. At ABC Widget Co., this screening interviewer is Heather Ogilvie. Let's get to know her a little bit.

Heather is a lower-level person in the personnel department (unless you are applying for a senior level job, in which case, she's received several promotions by the time she calls you) who has been given a rather bare-bones idea of the duties and responsibilities of the position for which you've applied. (That's not really *her* fault, since the person who will manage this new hire probably hasn't filled out a position description or done a good job telling Heather exactly what he's looking for.)

Heather's job is pretty simple: reduce the number of candidates whose resumes look right for an opening so they don't take up too much of the hiring manager's time.

After you have gone through the preliminaries with Heather, her end of the conversation will follow a script—she will be asking questions to see if you have the easily quantifiable qualifications for the position: the right degree, the right amount of experience, willingness to relocate, whatever.

Primarily, Heather will be trying to determine *if you've been truthful on your resume.* Did you work where and when you claim? Have the titles and responsibilities you're bragging about? Make the salaries you've stated?

The interview also will be somewhat qualitative: Do you exhibit sufficient enthusiasm for the position? Do you sound intelligent? Do you exhibit any obvious emotional disturbances? Are you articulate? Are you energetic? Are you a positive person?

The Trained Interviewer's Arsenal

If you pass the screening interviewer's first hurdles, you will face the arsenal of techniques she undoubtedly relishes. Remember, Heather is trained and practiced in the science of interviewing to a degree that has probably never been even dreamed of by the hiring manager—the person you're hoping to work for (unless, of course, you're applying for a job in the personnel department).

While it is the hiring manager who will indeed decide whether you'll still be checking the classifieds next week, Heather is the gatekeeper. You must get past her to get to the less scientific selection interview that will be conducted by your potential boss-to-be.

Let's start with what is, for most candidates, the worst possible test.

The Stress Interview

Anyone who's been through one of these never forgets it. Becoming increasingly common, the *stress interview* is designed to get past the pleasantries and the veneer and see what the candidate is *really* made of.

I was subjected to a stress interview before I'd ever heard of the technique—not the best way to prepare, believe me.

Some years ago, I applied for an editorial position at a major publishing company and made it past the first hurdle, a screening interview conducted in the corporate office.

Next, I was invited to come back to meet the director of personnel (yes, they called it "Personnel" back then). Her name was Carrie Hyman. Carrie greeted me pleasantly and led me back to her rather palatial office. We exchanged a few more pleasantries as I took my seat and settled in. Before I knew it, I felt as if I were undergoing a police interrogation in a country on Amnesty International's Top Ten list.

Assuming that I had been spoken of highly by the screening interviewer, I was shocked when Carrie began questioning my credentials, sarcastically soliciting the reasons I had majored in liberal arts rather than something "practical," and asking me what in the world made me think that I could edit a magazine, even though I had been doing just that for years (and quite well, I should add).

Carrie's questions were fired quickly, and each successive question veered dizzyingly to a completely unrelated topic. One question would be about my work experience; the next, about what I did to stay fit; the next, about my favorite movie.

Carrie's questions did exactly what I later discovered they were *intended* to do—they made me feel confused, fearful, hostile. I behaved badly, answered as many questions as I could in monosyllables, avoided looking Carrie in the eye.

Needless to say, I was not offered the job.

While I will discuss specific questions and how to answer them throughout the rest of this book, I would like to present now some of the valuable lessons for *all* interview situations that I learned from my experience with Ms. Hyman:

- No matter how stressful the situation, *stay calm.* Never take your eyes from the interviewer. When he or she finishes asking a question, take a second or two to compose yourself, then answer.
- *Recognize the situation for what it is*—an artificial scenario designed to see how you react under pressure. The interviewer (probably) has nothing against you personally.
- *Don't get despondent.* It's easy to think that the interviewer has taken a strong dislike to you and that your chances are nil. That's not the case. The

stress interview is designed to see if you will
become depressed, hostile and flustered when the
going gets tough.

- *Watch your tone of voice.* It's easy to become sar-
  castic during a stress interview. Presuming you do
  not realize what the interviewer is up to, you'll
  assume he's lost his mind.

What Would Happen if Everyone Else Called in Sick and...?

Hypothetical questions like that (whose weirdness or
dastardliness are limited only by the interviewer's imagina-
tion)—and I'll tell you about more of them in chapter 9—will
alert you that you are about to undergo the increasingly
popular *situational interview.*

This technique is designed to measure the degree to which
candidates demonstrate traits deemed key to success on the
job.

These are questions to which you will have to devote a
great deal of thought. Again, it is a category of questions for
which your personal inventory will provide much help.

The Interview With the Hiring Manager

While the techniques we've discussed thus far are most
likely found in the arsenals of human resources professionals, the interview with the hiring manager is not a walk
in the park. In fact, the experience and interviewing talent of
the personnel professional can actually be a comfort to you.
Why?

Well, skilled interviewers will stay in charge of the situation and not let the process meander down some dead-end,

non-productive track. In addition, there is some predictability to the way they conduct interviews, even though they can draw on several types of techniques.

A Little Knowledge is a Dangerous Thing

On the other hand, the hiring manager is sure to lack some or *all* of the screening interviewers' knowledge, experience, skill—and predictability.

The reason for that is simple: The vast majority of hiring managers in Corporate America don't know what it takes to hire the right candidate. Most of them certainly have had *no* formal training in conducting interviews of any kind.

What's more, most managers conducting interviews are only slightly less comfortable than the candidates sitting across the desk from them.

This scant knowledge about proper hiring techniques is certainly not beneficial to managers. But it can be even worse for candidates!

For instance, a hiring manager might decide you are not the right person for the job simply because *he* didn't ask the *right* questions, asked *ambiguous* questions, or, worse yet, asked all the *wrong* questions.

In fact, many perfect candidates for jobs walk out the door, never to return, for no other reason than hiring managers' ineptness.

What Can You Do About That?

What you can do is prepare to put your best foot forward *no matter what the hiring manager does!* You must be prepared with answers to the 100 questions in the chapters that follow ("Tell me about yourself" in chapter 2 was question #1), even though the hiring manager might never ask them.

"Huh?," you're wondering right now. "Is this guy nuts? Do all that work for *nothing?*"

Hardly.

The chapters that follow will demonstrate that you will be aiming to give the hiring manager not a bare set of *facts* about you, but a *feeling* that you are the absolute best person for the job. Simply put, hiring managers are looking for information that will allow their intuition to take over. In other words, facts alone are not what the hiring manager is after in the interview.

Needless to say, this can be a rather elusive, hard-to-define goal for an interview. I think the best term that human resources types have invented in trying to define it is *organizational fit.*

If the hiring manager is a skilled interviewer, she will use techniques like the situational interview to get a sense of how the candidate will perform on the job. If he is unskilled, as is usually the case, he will be almost passively hoping that the candidate will do a certain "something" during the interview that will say to him, "Hey, pal, I'm the one for you."

That Certain Something

One time I was in the happy position of having no positions open at a magazine I was running. My boss, Alexander, the company's publishing director, called me. "Ron," he said, "I know you have no positions open right now, but I have this woman, Lynn Woods, in my office. She was referred to me by a friend. Maybe you just want to say hello?"

Even though I was up to my ears with work, I took some time to ask Lynn some preliminary questions—where she was working, what her strengths were, what she was looking for. I had planned to get her out of my office in five minutes, but ended up talking for about a half hour, during which time she told me about her terrific editing and writing skills, the jobs she'd held, and why she was looking to make a move.

She impressed me so much that when, a few months later, the managing editor spot opened up on my magazine, I called Lynn in for a more thorough interview. She got the job.

Lynn had impressed me so much during an interview for which I was very unprepared, that when a position opened up, she immediately came to mind as the best candidate for it.

Lynn had displayed those traits that I keep stressing, because they are the traits *employers* are always looking for, no matter *what* the job description says: confidence, enthusiasm, experience and dependability.

How to "Ace" *Any* Interview

- *Think of the interview as an adventure* rather than a tribunal, and try to enjoy it. Think of it as a long-awaited chance to meet that sports star, famous author or movie celebrity you've admired (even though a middle-aged hiring manager with a paunch and bald spot might not have quite the right image). Sure, you'll be nervous, but you'll want to demonstrate your interest and try to cultivate the interviewer's interest in you.

  I'm reminded of the story of a friend of mine, who was considering law school and took the LSAT's while he was making up his mind. He scored pretty badly, so he immediately signed up to take them again. But by the time the next test date rolled around, he'd decided to pursue another career option.

  He went ahead and took the LSAT's again anyway, thinking of them as an experience, an adventure (and, besides, he'd already paid the fee). He scored *200 points higher*. He certainly hadn't prepared more, but his attitude for taking the test was right—he felt no pressure, which allowed his mind to perform at its best.

- *Be enthusiastic* about the position, about your accomplishments, about what you've found out about the company and the job for which you are interviewing.

- *Be honest.* Express enthusiasm only about the things you are genuinely enthusiastic *about*. Phoniness will not sell the hiring manager or the screening interviewer on you.

- *Keep on smiling.* Sure, you're accustomed to giving people a big smile when you shake hands with them. In the interview, keep on smiling. A smile makes you appear agreeable and pleasant. And who wouldn't want to work with a pleasant and agreeable person like you?

- *Make lots of eye contact.* Have you ever known someone who wouldn't look you in the eye? You begin to wonder what that person has to hide. Make eye contact while you're shaking hands with the interviewer and frequently throughout the interview.

- *Don't stare* or make *continuous* eye contact—that would make anyone feel uncomfortable.

- *Be positive.* It's best to keep negative words out of your interview vocabulary to the extent possible. As we'll see when we discuss questions about your previous jobs, you must put a positive spin on such issues as your reasons for leaving, relations with your superiors, etc.

  Repeat to yourself one thousand times, "Be positive!" before you go on any interview. When rehearsing your answers to interview questions, take all of the negative words out.

- Don't let the hiring manager's lack of interviewing skill or preparedness keep you from shining. *Be confident enough and prepared enough* to take control of the interview if need be.

Chapter 4

What Have You Done With Your Life?

Perhaps the most popular category of interview questions are those related to the facts about a candidates' work experience. The reasons are quite simple: Many employers think that the past is prologue to your future—how well you might do in the positions they are trying to fill. And employers want to be sure that your changing jobs is not attributable to some deep, dark character flaw.

So, be prepared to be thoroughly grilled on this area. And, more importantly, be prepared to answer positively.

Here are the questions most likely to come up.

Accentuate the Positive

2. Why are you thinking about leaving your current job?

It's amazing how often this question is fatal to candidates. Obviously, no one wants to leave a job they are absolutely enchanted with. But, at the same time, it will do you absolutely no good to say something like, "Because I hate my boss's guts with every fiber of my being, and I lie awake nights wondering how much it would cost to put out a contract on him."

Instead, do some of what management consultants call "visioning." Imagine what the ideal next step in your career would be, then act as though you are interviewing for that very position.

For instance, you might reply, "I am interested in developing my accounting skills and taking on more financial management responsibilities. There is a great deal I enjoy about my current job, but my growth potential at Closely Held, Inc. is limited because of the size of the company and the fact that expansion is not a part of its current strategic plan."

Unless you have been fired or laid off, you must sound as if you are sitting in front of that interviewer because you seek more money, more responsibility, a bigger challenge, better opportunities for growth.

Out of Work, Not Out of Luck

3. Are you still employed at the last firm listed on your resume?

The old adage that it's harder to find a job when you don't already have one is true. Employers are suspect of *anyone* who is out of work, even during times when corporate America is rife with layoffs, as indeed it lately seems to be every five years or so.

If you *have* been fired or laid off, be truthful, but turn the potential negative into a positive.

Let's consider the case of Nick Dean. Nick, a hotel sales manager, did, indeed, have one of those bosses that engender in employees gruesome fantasies of committing murder or, at least, inflicting severe bodily harm. A petty tyrant, he took Nick and his other subordinates to task quite often—publicly and mercilessly.

One day, Nick finally had it. He blew up, screaming back at his boss...and bringing a quick firing down on his head.

Interviewing for another hotel sales job, Nick was asked about his current status. He bluntly answered, "I was fired."

When the stunned interviewer asked to hear more, Nick said, "My boss Joe and I just didn't get along, and, I must admit, I didn't handle the situation that well. We have such vast differences in style. I'm someone with a lot of initiative who likes to be trusted to do a good job. Joe was highly structured, a very control-oriented manager who wanted the details on every sales call in triplicate.

"I certainly understand the importance of call reports and log sheets and other sales management controls. I guess I interpreted some of Joe's quick demands for these things as a lack of trust, and I shouldn't have. I learned my lesson."

Nick's answer is a classic case of turning a negative into a positive.

Even the most fair-minded interviewers will think a firing or layoff is a sign of weakness for the candidate. (I've even heard an experienced executive recruiter say, "Oh, if she got laid off, there *must* be *something* wrong with her. Companies don't ever let *really* good employees go." Oh, would that were true!)

If *you* have such a "blemish" on your record, talk *less* about why you were terminated and *more* about what you've learned from it. And don't dwell on the negatives, such as what a rotten boss you had.

If you were laid off, or, as the British quaintly say, "made redundant," remember that you really don't have anything to be ashamed of. Say something like, "Yes, I was one of sixteen people laid off when sales took a slide." (This is an easy way out...presuming you were not in the sales department!)

Nobody Loves You When You're Down and Out

Companies are especially cautious about hiring people who have changed jobs repeatedly. That might not seem odd, until you consider the fact that they are *also* wary about hiring those who have been with the same company for years. Hence, consider which of these questions might come up in light of your particular job history.

---

4. **After being with the same organization for so long, don't you think you might have a tough time getting accustomed to another?**

Your answer, of course, is that this is no impediment to your future success. After all, even though you've been at the same company, you've been exposed to more than one boss, many subordinates and/or co-workers, and you've had the chance to observe the workings of other organizations with which you've been in contact.

In fact, you should sell the interviewer on the idea that your *proven loyalty* is a highly desirable characteristic.

---

5. **You've changed jobs quite frequently. How do we know you'll stick around if we hire you?**

---

6. **You've been with your current employer only a short amount of time. Is this an indication that you'll be moving around a lot throughout your career?**

These are tougher questions. The hiring process is an expensive, time-consuming one to which few companies or managers lovingly submit. They want to make sure that potential employees are not merely job-hopping.

In framing your reply, portray the position for which you are interviewing as your career's Promised Land. You can do this by either: 1) Stating that you had had some difficulty defining your career goals, but now you are quite sure of your direction; or 2) convincing the interviewer that you've left previous positions because that was the best way to increase your responsibilities and broaden your experience.

For instance, Sherri, who had had three jobs in the first six years after graduation, framed this clever reply which combines both techniques:

"All through college, I was convinced that I wanted to be a programmer. When, after a few months, I found that I was unhappy with my first job, I naturally blamed the company and the particular type of work. So, when an opportunity opened up at Lakeside Bank, I grabbed it. But soon after the initial euphoria with the new job wore off, I was unhappy again.

"But I noticed that I really enjoyed the part of my job that dealt with applications. I learned of the job in end-user computing at SafeInvest and went for it. I learned a great deal there, but I hit the 'glass ceiling' pretty quickly there. There was no place to go because it's such a small firm.

"I was recruited for the applications position at DeepPockets Bank and got it because of some of the innovations I'd developed at SI. The work has been terrific, but once again I find that I'm a one-person department.

"The position for which I'm interviewing with you holds out the possibility of managing a department, interacting with programmers and applications specialists on the cutting edge. Learning is what makes working the most fun for me. This job would give me the chance to learn so much."

Are You Management Material?

Fortunately or unfortunately (depending on your point of view), moving up at most companies and in most careers means managing people.

If you are interviewing for a supervisory position or for a job that usually results in a promotion to management, the interviewer will try to get some feeling for your management capabilities.

---

7. **Have you managed people in any of the positions you've held?**

It's best to answer yes. Candidates with experience in managing other people will be considered more mature and be able to demonstrate that other employers have placed confidence in them.

If you haven't actually had people "reporting to you," talk about experiences you've had in which building consensus and working in teams were essential. If these experiences have convinced you that you have the right stuff to be a good manager, say so.

Candidates with management experience should tell the interviewer how many people they've supervised and in what capacities these people have worked.

---

8. **Have you been in charge of budgeting, approving expenses, and monitoring departmental progress**

against financial goals? Are you very qualified in this area?

Again, having responsibilities for setting budgets, approving expenditures, and monitoring income and expenses is a sign of other employers' faith in you.

If you've actually had no fiscal duties before, be truthful, but creative. For example: "Well, I've never actually run a department, but I've had to set and meet budgetary goals for several projects I've worked on. In fact, I did this so often that I took a class in Lotus 1-2-3."

If you've had broader fiscal responsibilities in your current or previous positions, talk about your approval authority (the largest expenditure you could sign off on) and, in round figures, the income and expenses of departments you've supervised.

---

9. How long have you been in the job market?

Of course, unless you've been fired or laid off, you should say that you've just started looking recently. If you think the interviewer has some way of knowing that you've been in the market for a while (perhaps you've come to him through a recruiter who knows your history), be prepared to explain why you haven't received any offers. Try to be sure these responses don't make you seem like an undesirable candidate.

---

10. Why haven't you received any offers so far?

Make yourself look desirable, *if you can do so truthfully.* "Oh, of course, I *have* had an offer, but the situation was not right for me. I'm especially glad that I didn't accept since I now have a shot at landing this position."

It's important to be truthful, because the interviewers next logical question is:

---

11. Who made you the offer? For what type of position?

If you lied when answering the previous question, you're in hot water now! Interviewers are likely to know a great deal about their competitors and what positions they're trying to fill.

If you did the smart thing and told the truth, give the interviewer the name of the company. It's *very* important to stress that the position you turned down was quite similar to the one you're applying for at this interviewer's firm. After all, if the job you're interviewing for here is "perfect for you"— as you've undoubtedly told the interviewer three or four times already—why would you be at all interested in something very different at the other company?

Tips for *Quantitative* Questions About Work

- *Be as positive as you can* about the reasons you're leaving your current job (or have left previous jobs). The key word here is *more* — as in *more* responsibility, *more* challenges, *more* opportunity and (but don't be obnoxious about it) *more* money.

- If you've been fired or laid off, *be as positive as you can* about the experience, and stress the lessons you've learned from it.

- Stress items in your background that **quantify** *the amount of confidence other employers have placed in you:* the number of employees you've supervised, the amount of money you controlled, the earnings that your department achieved.

- *Do not speak badly* of past supervisors or employers.

- *Shape your answers* so that the job for which you are interviewing sounds like a goal or a means to achieve your ultimate career objective. Be careful not to make it sound like a steppingstone or safe haven.

Chapter 5

Work and the "Real" You

While the quantitative data about your experience discussed in the last chapter (number of people supervised, amount of fiscal responsibility, current status) is important, both screeners and hiring managers will ask a number of additional questions designed to see what your experience says about the real you.

You will have to give a great deal of thought about these questions. In a sense, you will be asked to *assess your own career* so that interviewers can judge how well you might perform for them.

Strengths and Weaknesses

12. **What are your strengths as an employee?**

13. **Why should I consider you a strong applicant for this position?**

In chapter 1, I urged you to sit down with your data input sheets and cull from them lists of strengths, achievements and skills that make *you* the most qualified person for the position you're seeking.

If you fail to do this, questions like these almost surely will produce an audible gulp and an incoherent answer that won't further your efforts to take the next step in your career.

In thinking about how to answer questions like these, think about the description of the position. What strengths do you have that make you just right for that job? What accomplishments have you had that *prove* it?

---

14. **What are your biggest weaknesses as an employee?**

---

15. **What do you plan to do to correct those weaknesses?**

---

16. **What are the biggest failures you've had during your career?**

---

17. **What have you done to make sure they won't occur again?**

---

18. **What are the skills you most need to develop to advance your career?**

Remember: *The interviewer is not a priest, and his office is not a confessional!*

It would be absolutely foolhardy to provide a lengthy catalog of your shortcomings and disappointments just because someone asked you a question about your weaknesses or failures. But it would be equally silly to pretend you're perfect and have never experienced failure in the course of your career, education or life.

The best approach is a compromise: Admit to *one* weakness or *one* failure, but make it a *good* one! Then talk about the steps you are taking (or have taken) to make sure that you'll never fail in that way again.

For instance, if asked about your weaknesses, don't admit to any that the interviewer might naturally expect would hamper job performance, such as procrastination, laziness, lack of concentration. Instead, discuss a deficiency that might even be considered a plus, given the right "spin"—a tendency to take on too much yourself, a problem that you're trying to solve by delegating more; an impatience with work delays, which you're trying to overcome by getting a better understanding of all of the processes a finished product must go through; workaholism, which you're doing your best to remedy by reading time management books.

Also, try to think of a failure that took place relatively *early* in your career and/or one that would seem completely unrelated to the work you would be performing for your new employer. These questions might also be phrased this way:

---

19. **What do your supervisors tend to criticize most about your performance?**

---

20. **How did you do on your last performance appraisal? What were the key strengths and weaknesses mentioned by your supervisor?**

Likes and Dislikes

While interviewers are trying to be as objective as possible, they will be basing at least some—probably most—of their hiring decision on their *feelings* about the employee. They will mention such things as "attitude" and "organizational fit." Here are some of the questions they will ask to help them get a feeling about whether or not you and the company are a good match:

---

21. Tell me about the best boss you've ever had.

---

22. Tell me about the worst boss you've ever had.

Talk about loaded questions! In answering question 22, you might dredge up a perfect description of the hiring manager sitting across the desk from you, while your answer to question 21 perfectly describes his corporate nemesis. (Of course, if that happens, you probably wouldn't want to work for that hiring manager, but you might well want to check out openings in his enemy's department!)

Most companies, however, would want to hear that you have most enjoyed working for a boss who was very involved in monitoring your progress, was unselfish with her knowledge, and didn't hog all the credit.

I hope you've had the chance to work for someone like that, particularly if she also ran her department rationally and fairly—set reasonable goals, monitored progress frequently, and measured results objectively.

Asked to describe your worst boss, resist the urge to portray him as Saddam Hussein and, more importantly, don't introduce ideas into the conversation that might lead to questions about your competence or ability to get along with other people.

For instance, charges of "favoritism" might lead the interviewer to wonder why that boss liked others and not you. Alleging that this worst boss was "always looking over your shoulder" might lead the employer to wonder what it is that you were trying to hide.

Again, make sure that negatives you must discuss during the interview accentuate the positives about you. If you say that your boss was "selfish with his knowledge," you are implying your desire to learn. Likewise, saying that a supervisor was "uninvolved" could indicate your desire to work within a cohesive team.

---

23. Looking back on the experience now, do you now think there was anything you could have done to improve your relationship with that one bad boss?

Of course you do. The work experience you've had since has shown you how to accept criticism better, how to understand the pressures supervisors are under, how to better anticipate their needs. Use this opportunity to demonstrate your experience, perceptiveness and maturity.

Questions of Style

Do you have "style"?

This voguish term in business lingo has nothing to do with the way you dress. Rather, it encompasses how you conduct yourself on the job, the way you get along with superiors, subordinates and peers, the way you manage people, the way you like to be managed.

While the way you dress for a job interview is certainly important, the interviewer will be more concerned with these other elements of "style."

---

24. How do you go about making important decisions?

You should shade your answer to match the obvious characteristics of the type of person the company wants to hire.

For instance, if you're going to work for a financial services company, you probably don't want to portray yourself as a manager who makes decisions based on "gut feel," since such a company will probably want decisions that are supported with reams of data. At the same time, if you are auditioning for an air-traffic controller position, it's best not to say that you like to "sleep on things" before making up your mind.

The interviewer is asking this question to get some sense of your thoroughness, your analytical skills, your willingness to call on the expertise of other people, and your creativity.

---

25. Do you work well under pressure?

Naturally, everyone will say yes to this question. However, it will be best to provide examples that support your bragging about your cool head under fire. Be sure to choose anecdotes that don't imply that the pressure resulted from *your* procrastination or failure to anticipate problems.

---

26. Do you anticipate problems well or merely react to them?

Show the interviewer how good you are by anticipating and preparing for this *question!* All managers panic from time to time, but the best ones do so less frequently because of their ability to see problems around the bend.

For instance, one sales manager I know had his staff provide reports on all positive and negative budget variances weekly. This helped him provide valuable information not only to his boss, but also to the manufacturing, distribution, and marketing arms of the company, helping to improve product turnover and flagging sales. Such an anecdote is terrific fodder for successful interviews.

27. Would you describe yourself as a risk-taker or someone who plays it safe?

The ideal candidate, in most cases, will be a little of both. Interviewers asking this question are testing for innovation and creativity, to see whether you are a leader or a candidate for shearing. However, they are also probing to find out if you might be a "loose cannon" who will ignore company policies and be all-too-ready to head off into uncharted waters.

If You Had Your Druthers...

Interviewers use hypothetical questions to get candidates to drop their guards. Since most applicants will be well rehearsed on the facts of their careers and education, interviewers will ask them questions tied less directly to employment data in an attempt to draw them out:

28. If you could start your career all over again, what would you do differently?

29. What is the biggest mistake you ever made in choosing a job? Why?

Unless you're shooting for a complete change of career, you must convince the interviewer you have a great deal of affinity for your work and career moves were well thought out.

But that certainly doesn't mean that you can't have regrets. Did you leave your first job because you were too impatient for a promotion, only to realize you hadn't learned all you could have? Did you miss the opportunity to specialize in some area or develop a particular expertise that, in hindsight, you should have?

It certainly wouldn't be advisable to say something like, "I wish I had never gotten into magazine publishing in the first place, but now I guess I'm stuck. Darn, I could have been editing garden books for FernMoor Press."

Better to reply: "My only regret is that I didn't go in this direction sooner. I started my career in editorial, and I enjoyed that. But since getting into marketing, I can't wait to get to work every day."

---

30. Do you prefer to work with others or by yourself?

---

31. Are you good with people?

---

32. How do you get along with superiors?

---

33. How do you get along with co-workers?

---

34. How do you get along with people you've supervised?

Again, the position for which you are interviewing should dictate how you shape your answers. For instance, if you are interviewing for a job as an on-the-road, far-flung sales representative, you won't want to say that you thrive on your relationships with co-workers, and can't imagine working without a lot of interaction.

Less obvious is the answer that will convince interviewers that you are now, or one day will be, management material.

The most effective way to answer this type of question is to posit it in a work situation.

For instance: "When I'm faced with having to make an important decision, I rely on the advice of others. But *I'm* the one who has to consider all that's been said and *decide*. I guess that's why they say it's lonely at the top, because the higher you go in management, the more responsibility you have, the more you have to decide things by yourself."

Also, don't paint your work environment as a bed of roses without thorns. The old saying, "You can choose your friends, but you can't choose your relatives," is incomplete: Often you can't choose your co-workers either.

Every job situation forces us to get along with people we might not choose to socialize with. But we must get along with them, and, quite often, get along with them for long stretches of time under difficult circumstances.

Acknowledge this, and talk about how you've managed to get along with a *wide variety* of other people.

Once I was interviewing candidates for a production department manager position that had 16 people reporting to it. I had to gauge the "people skills" of the applicants very delicately, as production departments in publishing companies are filled with some of the quirkiest people (to be kind) you'll ever come across.

I asked the successful candidate a couple of the questions aimed at probing his management and communication skills. Finally, he gave me a firm glance and said, "Look, you know and I know that it's not always easy to manage artists and proofreaders. I do my best to convince them of the importance of deadlines. I talk to them about what it costs us when we blow deadlines and point out how unfair it is to others in the department and to the entire operation to hold things up.

"I usually find some way to get along with all of the people in the department, some way to convince them that timeliness and accuracy are absolute musts. It's not always easy, but a lot of times it's fun.

"When we are rushed because of another department's lateness, I use this as an object lesson. The most important thing is to distribute the work fairly and let everyone *know* that you are being fair and that you expect them to do their share."

Tips for *Qualitative* Questions About Work

- Interviewers using these questions will be asking you to evaluate your career and job performance. *Be honest, but* don't give away information that could come back to haunt you.

- Introduce only information and opinions that you think will be thought of as *positive.* If you have to talk about negative experiences, point out what you learned from them and why they won't happen again.

- *Strike a balance* between portraying yourself as a "company man (or woman)" and a "loose cannon." Screeners and hiring managers often like risk-takers, but they also put some stock in playing by the rules.

- *Use work situations* to illustrate your point as much as possible. These questions are asking that you be very subjective. Using concrete examples will keep you from drifting into vague generalities.

- *Choose your words carefully.* Make sure that you are indeed answering questions, and *not* suggesting other areas the interviewer should explore. For instance, I suggest, "I am looking for greater challenges," rather than, "The boss didn't give me enough to do."

Chapter 6

What Exactly Do You *Do* for a Living?

In most prizefights, the first round or two are relatively boring—the contestants "feel each other out," trying to get a sense of each other's feints and jabs, before the serious pummeling begins.

Likewise with most interviews. First the pleasantries, then the "getting-to know-you" questions, and then, if the interviewer thinks it worthwhile, the questions that separate the mere also-rans from the real contenders.

Let's Get Serious

Sure, some of the questions you've read about in chapters 3, 4 and 5 have been tough, but the answers to the questions in this chapter (as well as those in chapters 7, 8 and 9) will really help the interviewer get a handle on whether you can do the job.

---

35. **What were your most memorable accomplishments on your last job?**

36. What have been the most memorable accomplishments of your career?

Think about the position for which you're interviewing, then decide which accomplishments are most relevant.

For instance, when a friend of mine who had been an editor for years was asked this question, she talked about the times she'd been asked to write promotional copy by the marketing department. The reason: She was trying to change careers and get into advertising copyrighting.

Also, give a lot of thought to *why* you were able to achieve these peaks in your career—"I really stopped to listen to what my customers wanted, rather than just trying to sell them;" "I realized that I needed to know a lot more about Subchapter S corporations, so I enrolled in a tax seminar."

This will demonstrate that you give a great deal of thought to accomplishing your goals, that you were able to assess your shortcomings and find the means to correct them.

If the interviewer poses question 36 rather than question 35, focus primarily on accomplishments *at your current position,* perhaps with one look back to the job immediately preceding it or college days (if your current job is your first). What you're doing *now* (or what you did on the job you just left) is a key reason why the interviewer is considering you in the first place.

37. Was there anything your company (or department) could have done to be more successful?

Of course there was, but all of the things that could have been done were out of your control!

But don't just make up an answer that gets you off the hook. Demonstrate that you have a good feel for your business and have come up with possible solutions that, because of circumstances over which you had no control, could not be implemented.

A perfectly acceptable answer would be: "Sure, we could have expanded our product line, perhaps even doubled it, to take advantage of our superior distribution. But we just didn't have the capital and couldn't get the financing."

---

38. What is the title of the person to whom you report, and what are his or her responsibilities?

Aha! Gotcha!

If you've been exaggerating the responsibilities of your position, you're about to be found out. Don't portray your job as so big that there couldn't be anything left for your boss to do. This is a very common tendency among candidates. They might also be found out by:

---

39. Describe the way your department is organized.

Are You an Innovator?

---

40. Did you inaugurate any new procedures (or systems or policies) in any of the positions you've held?

Remember that most employers are looking for employees that are problem solvers. This question might very well be asked after you've described some of the reasons you're leaving your current job.

A savvy interviewer's natural tendency will be to wonder why, if something was broke, you didn't try to come up with a way to fix it.

What Will Become of You?

41. If you don't leave your current job, what do you think will happen to you in your career?

Even though you might not be able to bear the thought of staying in your present job for another minute, handle this question with what athletes call "soft hands."

Of course, you don't want to make everything at ABC Widget seem hopeless—"I think I'd rather hawk peanuts at the stadium than stay there another three months"—so convince the interviewer that you're the type of employee capable of making the most of any situation, even an employment situation you've just said you want to leave.

Your answer should be something like this: "Naturally I'm interested in this job and have been thinking about leaving ABC. However, my supervisors think highly of me, and I expect that one day other situations will open up for me at the company. I'm one of ABC's top salespeople. I have seen other people performing at similar levels advance to management positions. And that's what I'm looking for right now."

42. How far do you expect to advance with your current company?

A variation on the question above, this one again should be given a very positive, optimistic reply, one that connotes that you're happy to stay with ABC forever.

There is an old adage in job hunting: "There's no better time to look for a new job than when you're happy with your old job." The reason: You won't rush into anything. You will take the time to choose the job that's not just suited to you, but one that's downright *perfect* for you.

Therefore, it's best to conduct your part of the interview as if you are in the driver's seat, just cruising along happily until you have a chance to improve your career.

At the same time, you can't afford to be flip and make it seem that you're thinking, "I'm just waiting to find a company that's good enough for me."

Begin your answer to questions like this with the phrase, "Well, assuming I'm not the successful candidate for this position..."

If You're So Smart, How Come You're Not Rich?

While it is good to convince that employer that the world is your oyster and you're waiting for the perfect pearl of a job, you might get hit with questions like these:

---

43. **If you're so happy at your current firm, why are you looking for another job?**

---

44. **Your history of promotions and salary increases is good. Will they be surprised that you're leaving?**

Okay, so that mask you've been wearing—the one with the big, complacent grin on it—has just crashed to the floor. What do you do? After all, you've been telling the interviewer how much your employer loves you and how much you enjoy what you do for a living. So, why *would* you want to leave?

Even though you might want to leave because you hate the company, think it might go out of business at any second, or because you just broke off your engagement with the person sitting in the office next door, be positive in your reply.

The employer, remember, knows that you want to leave your current job and might be thrilled at the opportunity to hire someone with your terrific qualifications. The interviewer doesn't really *care* why you're leaving. He cares about what your decision to leave says about your attitudes about work, your loyalty, and how the employer feels about you.

So, come up with *a list of good reasons to leave* your current job—not good for you, but in terms of how the prospective employer will view your decision.

- You want more ***responsibility.***
- You want to expand your ***knowledge.***
- You've heard so many wonderful things about Good Times, Inc., that you wanted to explore this ***unexpected opportunity*** to work there.

Notice that there is not *one* negative word in any of these replies. You shouldn't say, "There is *no* room for me to move up at Grin & BearIt, Inc.," or "I can't get a promotion unless somebody dies." Bringing up negatives will lead any good interviewer to a much harder question.

---

45. If you have these complaints about your present company, and they think so highly of you, why haven't you brought your concerns to their attention?

Some problem-solver *you* are! You can't even talk to your boss about changes that might make you happier!

If you do lead an interviewer to ask you this question, your reply should be as positive as possible. "Grin & BearIt is aware of my desire to move up. But they're such a small company, there's not much they can do about it. The management team is terrific. There's no need right now to add to it, and they are aware of some of the problems this creates in keeping good performers. It's something they talk about quite openly."

More Tips for Interview Success

- ***Learn as much as you can*** about the position for which you are interviewing so that you can shade your responses appropriately. Mention accomplishments, the things you like best about your current job, etc., that will convince the interviewer you are suited to the demands of the position you want at his or her company.

- When formulating answers about accomplishments and failures, think not only in terms of *what,* but also *why.* Make the reasons for these things positive and ***stress the lessons*** you've learned that you can apply in your next position.

- ***Do not exaggerate*** your accomplishments or responsibilities. A savvy interviewer can find you out easily.

- Unless you've been terminated, make it seem that ***you're not desperate*** to get a new job. However, don't be smug. You must come across as interested in the employer's position for all those reasons that start with "more"—*more* responsibility, *more* knowledge, *more* opportunity.

- ***Avoid mentioning negative aspects*** of your current job. You want the interviewer to associate as few negative words or feelings with you as possible.

- Make it seem as if you might be able to find some of the things you're looking for in your current position. This will help convey the impression that you are a ***positive worker*** who tries to make the best of any situation.

- *Build a vocabulary of positive action words* that will spring to mind as you're responding to the interviewer's questions. You should use these and other positive words in your resume, in your job-hunting and follow-up letters, during the entire interview process, and...in every business letter you write for the rest of your life.

Here's the list. Read it over every day. Build some of it into the little speech about yourself we discussed in chapter 2:

Ability	Generated	Promoted
Achieved	Guided	Recommended
Accelerated	Initiated	Revised
Accurate	Implemented	Reorganized
Analyzed	Introduced	Responsible
Capable	Improved	Streamlined
Conceived	Launched	Strengthened
Conceptualized	Lead	Solved
Determined	Managed	Supervised
Developed	Monitored	Systematic
Directed	Motivated	Tested
Effective	Organized	Thorough
Energy	Planned	Trained
Enthusiasm	Prepared	Updated
Established	Presented	Urgency
Evaluated	Prided	Utilized
Excelled	Proficiency	Vital
Focus	Programmed	

Chapter 7

How Can the
Interviewer be Sure?

This is a classic good-news/bad-news scenario.

First, the good news: If you make it beyond some of the questions we've posed in chapters 4, 5 and 6, the interviewer probably likes you. Almost all screening interviewers and most hiring managers can eliminate candidates they are positive wouldn't work out long before they get to the questions in this and the following chapters.

Now, the bad news: The interviewer will want to make *sure* you're a good catch. So, he'll either call you back for another interview (which is standard operating procedure these days) or continue grilling you when your defenses and the facade you've been holding up finally start to flag.

The Gold Ring

46. What interests you most about this position?

Of course, the reasons have to do with greater responsibilities and challenges, bigger growth opportunities, the chance to supervise more people, the chance to develop a new set of skills while sharpening those you've already learned.

You know the drill from some of the previous chapters. However, here you should also take the time to show that you have taken some time to learn about *this* prospective employer and the *specific* position you're competing for.

Do some homework to find out about the prospective employer's business. Get the answers to these questions:

- What are the company's leading products? What products will it be looking to introduce in the near future?
- What are the company's key markets? How strong are they? What's the company's share of each market?
- What are the company's prospects for growth and expansion?

The answers to these questions will help *you* formulate the right answers to the interviewer's questions.

For instance, your reply might go something like this: "I've heard so much about your titanium ball bearings that I have wanted to experiment with different applications for them." Much better than saying, "I will have a better commute if I get this job," an answer that I have heard from more than one interviewee when I've asked that question!

Do Some More Homework

Doing some preliminary research also will provide you a leg up should the interviewer ask:

47. What do you like most about our company?

48. What have you heard about our company that you *don't* like?

If asked question 48, give an answer that doesn't relate directly to your job. For instance, you might have heard that ABC Widget had a layoff 12 months ago, prompting you to wonder if the dust has settled. Or you might have heard a rumor of a merger.

While you must be tactful in answering this question, don't play dumb. Undoubtedly you will have reservations about *any* prospective new job.

If the interviewer opens the door for you to ask what might otherwise be uncomfortable questions, by all means take advantage of it.

49. What about the job we've described to you has the *least* appeal?

Gulp!

This is another tough question that demands an answer other than, "Oh, everything about this job sounds just hunky-dory."

There is an old joke (which we hope won't offend any of our readers): An Irishman is speaking to a friend, who in consternations says, "Why do you Irish always answer a question with a question?" The Irishman, taken aback, thinks for a moment and replies, "Do we now?"

Your best tactic is to do as the Irishman in the joke does: Shoot a question right back at the interviewer.

For instance: "You've described a position in which I'd be overseeing some extraordinary levels of output. What sort of quality-control procedures does this company have? Are there QC specialists in-house with whom I'll be able to consult?"

In the Best of All Possible Worlds

---

50. Describe your ideal job based on what you know
about our industry right now.

---

51. How does that ideal stack up against the description
of the job you're applying for?

The ideal job is one in which you will have a broad scope of
responsibilities that will enable you to continue to learn about
your industry and grow. So use your knowledge about the
industry to formulate a reply that will sound idealistic, but not
unrealistic.

For instance: "I know that many accounting firms are
deriving more and more of their fee income from consulting
services. I would like a job that combines my cost-accounting
knowledge with client consultation and problem-solving.

"I'd like to start doing that as part of a team and eventually head up a practice in a specific area. My favorite disci-
pline is cost-accounting in manufacturing environments."

Based on what you know about the current position, describe the similarities, describe one (and *only* one) of the
shortcomings, if there are any, and formulate some questions
about unknown aspects of the position.

For instance, to continue from our example above: "I know
this position is in the auditing area and that you hire many of
your entry-level people into that department. I must confess I
would like this to be a steppingstone to working more in the
manufacturing area and, several years down the line, in
consulting. I'm sure I don't have the requisite knowledge or
experience yet. Is this a position in which I can gain such
experience, and is this a career track that's possible at this
firm?"

Up With People

---

52. What types of people do you find it most difficult to get along with?

What a land mine *this* could be! You might say, "Pushy, abrasive people," only to find out the interviewer is a born-and-bred stereotypical New Yorker (just kidding).

So, as is the case with these and other questions designed to evaluate your compatibility, be tactful in your answers. In other words, don't say *any*thing that any hiring manager could conceivably object to.

One candidate I interviewed gave me what I thought was a perfect answer to this question. After thinking about it for five seconds, she replied, "I have a problem that I was discussing with my boss just the other day. He told me I'm too impatient with slow performers, that the world is filled with 'C', rather than 'A' or 'B' people, but I expect them all to be great performers. So, I guess I *do* have trouble with mediocre and poor workers."

---

53. Are there any people that have trouble getting along with you?

This is a tough one! If you say no, the interviewer will know you're being evasive. So, once again, you must have a ready answer, hopefully one that no company would find objectionable.

I suggest thinking of an anecdote that might make the reasons for someone disliking you humorous. For instance, when a colleague of mine was asked this question on a job interview, he remembered the first position he held. He got a job with a state agency, the first new hire his department had

had in six years. Just out of college, Geoff was a go-getter. He worked at twice the speed of his peers, and they hated him for it. This provided him a ready-made answer to this question, one that made him look good.

Hiring and Firing

54. Have you ever hired anyone?

55. Why did you choose him or her (or them)?

If you *did* hire someone—or many people—during your career, your answer could go something like this: "Yes. I've hired people, and I've decided on whether or not some internal applicants were right for my department. The first time I hired someone, I looked to see that she had *all* of the right qualifications. I just went down the checklist. Since then, I've learned that some candidates who became excellent workers didn't necessarily have every qualification on that checklist, but they more than make up for whatever they lacked with enthusiasm and a willingness to work with other people."

If you *have not* ever hired someone: "Not really. But on several occasions I was asked my opinion about applicants. Of course, in those cases, I was trying to determine whether or not that person would be a team player and if he or she would get along with the other people in the department."

56. Have you ever fired anyone?

57. What caused you to fire that person?

If you *did* fire someone, I'm sure you had good reasons, although no firing is pleasant.

Think about the circumstances for the dismissal and provide a sanitized, brief version of the events to the interviewer. Remember, you don't want to seem like a negative person. And ragging on a poor, out-of-work subordinate will surely make you seem like one.

For instance, if you fired someone for not meeting productivity goals, you might be *thinking,* "Boy, I'm glad I got rid of that bum Evan. He was nothing but a simp and whiner who never did a good day's work." But you should *say* something like this: "Yes, I fired someone who continually fell short of his productivity goals. His shortcomings were documented and discussed with him for months, but he failed to show any real improvement. I had no choice. As a supervisor, you want everyone to work out, but, let's face it, not everyone is as dedicated to his or her job as we'd like."

If you have *not* actually fired anyone: "I never actually fired anyone myself, but it was the policy at my company that no hirings or firings should be unilateral. I was asked on two occasions to give my opinions about someone else's performance. It's never easy to be honest about a co-worker's shortcomings, but I had to do what was best for the department and fair to everyone else."

And Now, a Word From Our Inner Selves

---

58. What does the word "success" mean to you?

---

59. What does the word "failure" mean to you?

These questions should be taken to be both personal and job-related. If your definitions of success and failure involve only your job, you might seem to the interviewer to be little more than an automaton. However, if you mention only the goals you have in your personal life, it will seem as if you are not sufficiently concerned with success on the job.

Strike a balance. For example, this might be your answer to the question on success: "I have always enjoyed supervising a design team. In fact, I've discovered that I'm better at working *with* other designers than actually designing myself. And, unlike a lot of the people in my field, I'm able to relate to the requirements of the manufacturing department.

"So, success would mean working with others to come up with designs that *work* and that can be up on the assembly line quickly. Of course, the financial rewards of managing a department provide me the means to travel during my vacations. That's the thing I love most in my personal life."

It is better to use an example to demonstrate what you mean by "failure;" otherwise, you might get into a lengthy philosophical discussion more suited to a Bergman film than an interview.

Here's a good answer: "Failure is not getting the job done when I had the means to do so had I acted differently. For instance, once I was faced with a huge project. I should have realized at the outset that I didn't have the time—were there 48 hours in a day?—or the knowledge to do it correctly. I should have sought the help of others in my department and not been afraid to ask for help. That won't ever happen to me again if I can help it."

Yes, Everyone Hates This Question

When people become parents, they can't believe they're telling their kids some of the same things their parents said to them—"If your friends jumped off a bridge, would you do that, too?" Similarly, when they get the chance to interview job candidates, they will ask some of the same dumb questions that made them groan in years past. Here's the worst of the lot:

---

60. What do you want to be doing five years from now?

Or

---

61. What do you want to accomplish in your life?

Or even

---

62. What are your most important long-term goals?

Of course, you want a position of responsibility in your field, but you can't appear to be "too pushy" or overly ambitious.

So, start out your answer humbly: "Well, the ultimate answer to that question will depend mostly on my individual performance on the job and partly on the growth and opportunities offered by my employer."

Then, toot your own horn a little bit: "I've demonstrated leadership characteristics in all of the jobs I've held. So I feel confident that I will have continually greater management responsibilities in the future. And that suits me fine. I enjoy building a team, developing its goals, and working to accomplish them. It's very rewarding."

---

63. Have you recently established any new objectives or goals?

This question provides you an opportunity to demonstrate how your goals and motivations have changed as you've matured and gained valuable work experience. If you've recently become a manager, talk about how that has affected your outlook on your future career. If you've recently realized that you must sharpen a particular skill to continue growing, mention that.

Do You Have What it Takes?

64. How would you describe your management philosophy?

If asked, you want to assure the interviewer that you'll be neither a pushover nor a dictator. You also want to demonstrate a desire and ability to delegate, teach, and distribute work fairly.

Don't use some of these rather wishy-washy answers that I've actually heard during interviews: "I try to get people to like me and then they really work hard for me;" and "I guess you could say I'm a real people person."

Instead, give an answer that gives the impression of authority and experience: "I think that management is, more than anything else, getting things done through other people. The manager's job is to do his best to provide the resources and environment in which people can work effectively.

"I try to do this by creating teams, judging people solely on the basis of their performance, distributing work fairly, and empowering workers, to the extent possible, to make their own decisions. I have found that this breeds loyalty and inspires hard work."

Convincing the Interviewer You're a Good Catch

- Do some *homework* about the company and, if possible, the position for which you will be interviewing.

- Give the interviewer strong answers that *demonstrate experience and confidence.* Use examples that are relevant to the position you're shooting for.

- *Be humble* when asked about future goals, but convey the impression that you have the ability to succeed should opportunities come along.

- When responding to questions about management philosophy and experience, *appear firm, but not dictatorial.* Convey the impression that you are able to delegate, while having a keen awareness of the work for which all of your charges are responsible.

- Convey to the interviewer the fact that you've grown within your jobs, that your *goals have changed* during your career as a result of new growth experiences.

- When asked about failures, talk about what you've *learned and changed* as a result of them. Provide at least one example.

- When asked about successes, you should, of course, talk about job-related situations, but don't give the impression that you're a soul-less automaton. Talk about *how it made you feel* and what effects it might have had on your personal life.

Chapter 8

Person to Person:
Is Anybody Home?

If you could, would you hire an android to work for you?

Probably not. Nevertheless, if you're like most candidates, your interview behavior will probably be something right out of "Lost in Space."

Most job candidates seem to think that someone who talks only about work, work, work will have the best chance to get the job. But talking about the nuts-and-bolts of your livelihood probably *won't* let that ineffable "real" you shine through.

As I've stressed, you must try to reveal the best aspects of your personality as you provide responses to even the most routine questions. And, of course, it's even more important to do that when asked what we will refer to as "personal questions."

But remember: personal questions are a double-edged sword. Answering them might lead you to introduce information that it's illegal for employers to ask about **unless you bring it up first.** For instance, you might not want to tell the employer that you're a single parent if you're applying for a job that involves occasional travel or 16-hour days.

So, while these questions will give you an opportunity to demonstrate what a terrific person you are, they could also provide employers information they shouldn't factor into their decisions.

To Your Good Health

65. Are you in good health?

66. What do you do to stay in shape?

These are becoming more important as employers watch their health insurance bills—and the costs associated with having someone out on sick leave—skyrocket.

Be honest in answering this one, as the background check done by your prospective employer's insurance carrier will reveal your entire medical history. Besides, many offers of employment these days are contingent on your passing a physical examination, so you might as well be up front now.

And if, like me, you're not an exercise nut, mention an activity that provides some health benefit, such as yard work, house repairs, running after the kids, etc.

67. Do you have any physical problems that may limit your ability to perform the job for which you're applying?

Yes, that's a legal question because it's related directly to job performance. Answer it honestly.

Your Spare Time

68. What do you like to do when you're not at work?

Being careful, as always, to avoid introducing material you don't want to be asked about, present yourself as a well-rounded person. My answer to this question has combined a list of passive and active activities: playing piano, contract bridge, golf, movies, books, watching pro sports.

You must be careful not to portray yourself either as a not-too-swift couch potato ("I'm a baseball fan. I like to watch every game. I also like sitcoms.") or as someone so over-subscribed that you are headed for a collapse, probably soon after your new insurance coverage kicks in ("I play racquetball, coach a softball team, am on the board of directors of the local museum, plan to run for city council this fall, and, in my spare time, attend lectures on Egyptology at the university.").

Many employers subscribe to the theory, "If you want something done, give it to a busy person." So you want to portray yourself as an active, vital individual, but not someone who is driving himself to sure nervous exhaustion.

And shy away from mentioning interests that could cause a squeamish employer to envision a prolonged sick leave (skiing, rugby, etc.), or those that might be personally objectionable to the interviewer (work with Amnesty International, the Young Republicans, the Holy Roller Church). Rarely will any of these relate in any way to the job for which you're applying, so why are you opening a potential can of worms? (No, there's nothing wrong with being a Republican—or, for that matter, Amnesty International or church) but if you're interviewing with the Last of the Red Hot Liberals, why set yourself up to be rejected for something that has *absolutely* nothing *to do with the job for which you're interviewing?)*

Up Close and Personal

Skilled interviewers are able to ask questions that are sure to get you talking (from the examples above, "How did you get interested in contract bridge?") so that your guard will be low-ered and they can get to know the real you a bit better. They will then ask questions like these:

---

69. How would your co-workers describe you?

Of course, they would describe you as an even-tempered person who is a good team player. You have found that "a lot more can be accomplished when people gang up on a problem rather than on each other."

Remember that personal inventory I asked you to do in chapter 1? Well, this is where it will come in especially handy. Think back to the lists headed "Strongest Skills," "Greatest Areas of Knowledge," "Strongest Parts of My Personality," and, to a lesser degree, "Areas of My Personality That I Should Improve." These will provide ample words for you to put in your co-workers' or friends' mouths.

---

70. How do you generally handle conflict?

I hope that you can answer this question honestly this way: "I really don't get angry with other people very often. I'm usually able to work things out or anticipate problems before they occur. When conflicts can't be avoided, I don't back down, but I do try to be reasonable about it." Or: "Confronta-tions I've had in the workplace have been with those whom I don't feel are holding up their end of the job. Employees owe it to their bosses, customers and co-workers to do their jobs pro-perly."

---

71. How do you behave when you're having a problem with a co-worker?

In this case, relate an incident in which you *did* have trouble with a co-worker (and who doesn't from time to time?) and talk about what you learned from it.

For instance: "I had to work with this designer who was obstinate about listening to any of my suggestions. He would answer me in monosyllables and then drag his feet before doing anything I requested.

"Finally I said, 'Look, we are both professionals and neither of us has the right answer all the time. I notice that you don't really like my suggestions, but rather than being mulish about implementing them, why don't we just discuss what you don't like as two adults should?' "That worked like a charm. In fact, we actually became friends."

---

72. **If you could change one thing about your personality with a snap of your fingers, what would it be? Why?**

Talk about a trait listed in your weaknesses that you don't allow to get in the way of your work. You might say: "Boy, I had a bad time with procrastination in college, but I licked it because having to burn the midnight oil during exam week every semester was driving me nuts.

"Now, I must confess, I still have the *urge* to procrastinate (as you smile disingenuously) rather than just jumping right into things. I wish that I never felt like putting things off."

---

73. **Describe your best friend and what he or she does for a living.**

---

74. **In what ways are you similar or dissimilar to your best friend?**

These two questions are another way of saying, "So, tell me about yourself" now that you have your guard all the way down. Since the theory goes that best friends are very much alike, take pains to describe a person that the company would find easy to hire.

I Love Me. Who Do You Love?

Only the most annoying people *don't* find it difficult to talk about themselves in a flattering way. And that's what you'll be doing on the interview—constantly blowing your own horn until even *you* will want to change the tune.

You'll be saying what a great guy your friends think you are, what a pleasure your supervisors thought it was to have you on their team, that there are only a few little adjustments you'd like to make to your personality. Why, this can all sound pretty sickening.

When Things Get Personal

Don't get carried away with yourself. When you are answering these questions:

- Remember that companies are looking for these traits: *enthusiasm, confidence, energy, dependability, honesty, pride in work.*
- *Formulate answers that suggest these characteristics.* Think about what you would want in an ideal employee if *you* owned a company. Wouldn't you want problem-solvers, team players, people willing to work hard, people who enjoy what they are doing? So will the interviewers you'll be meeting— particularly the hiring managers.

For instance, a friend of mine had to work his way through college, holding down a number of menial positions totally unrelated to the career he hoped eventually to enter. He simply could not afford to participate in low- or no-pay internship programs or get involved in a lot of extracurricular activities. He had to pump gas or stock supermarket shelves during his summers.

This presented a difficult problem for him as he prepared for an interview at a publishing company for a job he coveted. Publishing is a very internship-oriented field, and many companies like to hire candidates who have spent their summers fetching coffee for editors and art directors.

My friend knew that questions about how he had spent his summer vacations would come up with his Ivy League interviewer. Therefore, he was prepared with answers like, "I wish I'd had more time to do things like work on the school paper, but whenever I wasn't studying, I pretty much had to work to pay for college.

"During all of those jobs, though, I learned a number of things that people learn only after they have been in their careers for a while, like how to work with others and how to manage time effectively."

Chapter 9

What if Everyone Called in Sick and...

Many of you will soon come face to face with an increasingly popular line of questioning, the so-called *situational interview*. Hypothetical questions like the ones posed in this chapter are geared to measure the degree to which candidates demonstrate traits someone has decided are necessary for success in a given position. They are supposed to measure candidates' resourcefulness, logic, conceptual thinking ability, and creativity.

Rather than trying to get a sense of who you are, interviewers asking such questions also are interested in trying to predict *how you'll perform* if you're the successful candidate for the job. How will they do this? By verbally conjuring up a series of real or hypothetical situations—none of which you can realistically predict or specifically prepare for—and asking how you'd behave in each one.

And So it Goes

While situational interview questions can come in many shapes and sizes, I'll give you a few selections in this chapter so that you will be at least somewhat prepared to provide excellent answers.

75. Your supervisor left an assignment in your "in" box, then left town for a week. You can't reach him and don't fully understand the assignment. What would you do?

Of course, you'd suck up the courage to approach your boss's supervisor to see if he or she could help you out. You would talk to him or her about the situation and tell him or her what *your* understanding of the assignment is.

You would tell the supervisor that because of your lack of familiarity with the company's procedures, you wanted to be sure that you had the assignment right.

And, of course, you would not do this in any way that would reflect badly on your boss's handling of the situation. You would explain that you and your boss simply missed the chance to talk to one another in her rush to complete all of her essential tasks before leaving the office.

What Do I Know?

76. The successful candidate for this position will be working with some highly trained individuals who have been with the company for a long time. How will you fit in with them?

Your answer should indicate a willingness—make that an *eagerness*—to learn from your future co-workers, rather than raise doubts about how they might react to you, the new kid on the block.

Convey the fact that you are bringing something to the party (skills, knowledge, insights into the competition), but that you realize you have a lot to learn from your prospective co-workers.

---

77. Your supervisor tells you to do something in a way you know is dead wrong. What would you do?

This is a tough question, so why not *acknowledge* that it is, with an answer like this: "Situations like this could force good employees to run the risk of seeming insubordinate. I would pose my alternative to my supervisor in the most deferential way possible. If he insisted that I was wrong, I guess I'd have to do it his way."

Oh No, Not That Again!

---

78. How will you handle the least interesting or least pleasant tasks that are part of this job?

An interviewer posing this question will usually build in specific aspects of the position, such as: "You won't always be looking for creative solutions to our clients' tax problems. Most of the time, you'll be churning out the returns and making sure you comply with the latest laws. You're aware of that, of course?"

Your answer should be something like this: "I'm sure that every job in the accounting field has its routine tasks (notice, I didn't say mind-numbingly boring) that must be done. Doing those jobs well is satisfaction in itself. The relatively infrequent chances we do get to be creative are extremely satisfying, of course, but we can't expect them to come along every day."

79. You've had little experience with budgeting (or sales or marketing or whatever). How do you intend to learn?

"Well, throughout my career, I've proven to be a quick study. For instance, when my company's inventory system became computerized, I didn't have the time to go through as much training as my peers. It was a difficult time in my department. But the company supplying the software had developed some computer-based tutorials and training manuals that I worked with when I could find some free time.

"I hope that I'd be able to do something similar to pick up the rudiments of your budgeting system."

80. This is a much smaller (or much larger) company than you've ever worked at. How do you feel about that?

If the company is larger, you are undoubtedly looking forward to terrific growth opportunities and exposure to more areas of knowledge than you have access to now.

If the prospective company is smaller, you are looking forward to a far less bureaucratic organization where decisions can be made much more quickly and where no department is so large that it is not extremely familiar with the workings of the entire company.

And So On

All situational interview questions will run along similar lines. Learn what you can about the position for which you're interviewing and anticipate the questions that might come up. As the samples I've included indicate, situational interview questions often are asked so that companies can get a good idea as to how quickly you will adapt to the new position and how you will learn skills that you might not already have.

For My Next Trick...

Interviewers also will shoot questions designed to measure how proficient you are in the skills they consider the most important to the job.

---

81. Are you an organized person?

Even if you firmly believe that "a neat desk is the sign of a sick mind," talk about the organizational skills that you do have—time management, project management, needs assessment, delegation.

---

82. Do you manage your time well?

I hope that you can truthfully say that you are a great self-starter and almost never procrastinate. Good employees are able to set goals, "prioritize" their tasks, and devote adequate, appropriate amounts of time to each.

However, in answering a rather conceptual question like this one (and what could be more conceptual than time?), try to sprinkle in specifics: "I rarely miss a deadline"; "I establish a 'To Do' list first thing in the morning and add to it as the day goes on;" "I love workplace interaction, but I try to set aside several interruption-free periods every day so I can pay close attention to detailed tasks, such as estimating."

How to Handle a Situational Interview

- *Avoid throwing the bull.* No type of interview technique invites candidates to be boastful, to exaggerate, or to downright *fabricate* more than the situational interview. But no other technique *exposes* that tendency in a candidate so effectively, either.

- Admit that a tough situation would make you nervous, might even lead you to momentary panic. *Honesty is the safest policy* when faced with this line of questioning.

- Show that you have *a grasp of the real world*, and that you realize that you have a lot to learn about your prospective new company. This will be much more effective than trying to present yourself as an Iacocca-like company savior.

- Think about how you'll answer questions about all such *hypothetical scenarios.* Assume these questions will be about areas of knowledge and skill you've yet to develop.

Chapter 10

There are No Innocent Questions

I'll never forget this story told to me by a friend, the head of recruitment for a rather large company. He had many weeks during which he would interview scores of candidates for various openings, so he became quite adept at immediately giving a quick hook to candidates he knew wouldn't work out.

His quickest "thanks for stopping by" of all time was delivered before he even had the chance to get the candidate back to his office. He asked the young woman, an applicant for a field sales position, simply, "How are you?" And the applicant immediately began whining about the fact that it was raining and she had a run in her stocking.

The recruiter turned to her and said, "Oh, are you here to apply for that field sales position? Oh, darn, we forgot to call. We filled it yesterday, but we'll keep you in mind for other similar positions that come along. Thanks for stopping by."

Watch What You Say

This example demonstrates an interview truism that few candidates realize: *There is no such thing as a meaningless question.* You are being judged from the moment the interviewer sees you (or hears you on the phone) until the offer of employments is made.

There are many examples of these seemingly innocent questions that can do you in. Here are a few:

---

83. (the aforementioned) How are you today?

---

84. Did you have any trouble finding us?

You are doing just great, thank you, and no, you didn't have any trouble at all because (you won't say this, you'll just do it) you took the time to get adequate directions from the interviewer's assistant.

Again, it all comes down to being positive. I'm not suggesting that you plaster some idiot grin on your face and warble "Don't Worry. Be Happy" as you skip down the hall, but *do* make every effort *not* to have negatives associated with *any* part of your interview.

I must admit that since my friend, the recruiter referred to above, told me his little story about the quick hook, I pay much more attention to the answers to these little throwaway questions. (Confirming, of course, that they are anything *but* throwaways.)

---

85. Do you know much about our company?

Believe it or not, many, many candidates simply answer "no" to this question, thinking it a mere "ice-breaker."

What a terrible thing to do! Why would you go into one of the most important encounters of your life so thoroughly unprepared? And then admit it!?

I have urged you to do your homework, and here is where the research you've done on the company will come in handy. Toss out a few salient (and positive) facts about the company, and finish off with a question that will put the ball back in the interviewer's court:

"Boy, what a growth story Starter Up is! Didn't I read recently that you've had seven straight years of double-digit growth? I saw in your annual report that you are planning to introduce a new line of products in the near future. I jumped at the chance to apply here. Can you tell me a little bit about this division and the position you're interviewing for?"

Is He Just Passing Time?

I've taken to asking some seemingly bizarre questions of job candidates and have read in the human resources literature that I'm not at all out of the ordinary.

Interviewers will try to get away from the more cliched interview questions, because, like the questions for a stolen exam, they might not really test candidates at all.

---

86. What's the last book you read?

Sure, that's one they ask in the Dewar's ads, but it does say a lot about a person. Nonfiction readers are interested in the world about them. Fiction readers seem to be interested in escape. Or, at least, that's how many interviewers will simplify it.

Think about a popular how-to book that you might discuss with the interviewer, regardless of your literary tastes. This will demonstrate that you're interested in "searching for excellence," "thriving on chaos" or going "up the organization."

87. What's the last movie you saw?

Mention a popular, noncontroversial movie. It won't do you a bit of good to say, "Last Tango in Paris," "Friday the 13th, Part 86," or even "Thelma & Louise" (unless you have a good reason that has *nothing to do with the movie's content.* I could note, for example, that my brother-in-law was the country-boy rapist in the latter movie, a good reason to have seen it!)"

But in general, do you want your taste in foreign films or left-wing documentaries to stand between you and a job? If you think it might and don't want it to, talk about that goofy Tom Hanks movie. If you think it shouldn't matter, then feel free to discuss your ideas on "Blue Velvet."

How to Avoid a One-Minute Interview

- Remember: *No question is a throwaway.* Give careful consideration to ALL of your answers.

- Again, think of those traits that employers are looking for most: *confidence, enthusiasm, dependability, and vigor.*

- Answer even seemingly innocuous questions carefully and *noncontroversially.* Why open up a can of worms...unless, of course, you'll willing to invite the interviewer to "go fishing?"

- Remember: *You're on a job interview,* not at a meeting of the local literary society or movie fan club. An answer that helps you get the job is preferable to one that accurately reflects your literary or cinematic tastes.

- The interview starts *the moment you walk in the door* (or pick up the phone).

Chapter 11

Going Back to School

At some point during your interviews, you probably will be asked about your college days. But the amount you will be asked about your education is in *inverse* proportion to the amount of real-world, on-the-job experience you have. (In other words, the more work experience you have, the less anyone will care about Boola Boola U.)

Therefore, much of this chapter will be geared to those relatively inexperienced readers who will be faced with the prospect of peddling their personalities and degrees, and, lacking real-world experience, little else.

What Did You Take Up in College, Besides Space?

88. **What extracurricular activities were you active in? What made you choose those? Which of them did you most enjoy? Why?**

You want to portray yourself as a well-rounded person. If you were not a member of many official school clubs or teams, talk about other activities you engaged in during college. Did you work part-time? Did you tutor other students? Did you do work to gain extra course credit?

Again, interviewers are looking for industrious people, not individuals who do just enough to eke by. This is *not* a good place to joke "Well, I didn't do much but drink beer on weekends, John," especially if it were true! (I could make a case that there is *never* a particularly good time or place to joke during an interview—one person's innocent joke is another's reason—stupid and unfair or not—to reject a candidate!)

---

89. What led you to select your major? Your minor?

---

90. Which courses did you like most? Which courses did you like least?

If you were strictly a liberal arts major, talk about the skills you developed in some of your courses: writing ability, debating skills, language skills.

Regarding your favorite courses, focus on those that are career-oriented, assuming that you took courses related to the job at hand.

When asked about your least-favorite courses, of course, you will pick one *not* related to your eventual career. Try to develop answers that have to do with the *subject*, rather than such things as the professor's personality or the workload in the course. Talking about troubles with an authority figure will introduce a possible negative into your candidacy. And, of course, complaining about too much work is always a terrible thing to do.

---

91. If you were to start college over again tomorrow, what courses would you take? Why?

Think about changes that you would make in your course selections that would have produced a better candidate *for that job*. Should you have taken more marketing courses, an accounting course, a statistics seminar?

Don't say, for instance, that you would have gone away to school so that you could date more. At the same time, don't be afraid to admit that it took you a little while to find the right course of study, then talk about how valuable courses "unrelated" to your career were in your development.

92. What are your most memorable experiences from college?

Talk about an experience related to the job at hand. It might be very touching that you met your best friend for life in college, but it will hardly seem relevant to the interviewer.

Experience of a Sort

93. What did you learn from (or why don't I see any) internships on your resume?

Interviewers will probe relatively inexperienced candidates to see how "trainable" they are.

No company really believes that someone is going to come out of college or graduate school and be immediately productive.

If asked this question, stress how the real-world internship experience complemented the academic training you had received.

However, never pretend that college is where you learned the secret of life. No interviewer is going to react favorably to a young whipper-snapper who acts like he knows it all.

94. In what courses did you get your worst grades? Why? How do you think that will affect your performance on the job?

Many companies will ask to see copies of inexperienced candidates' college transcripts, so you might as well spill the beans now!

If you flunked every accounting course and have even a modicum of intelligence you're probably *not* applying for an accounting job, right? *Right?*

So, hopefully, you can blame the bad grades you might have received in some of your electives to the amount of time and effort you were putting into your major.

Special Tips for Recent College Grads

- Don't be afraid to tell the interviewer that *you'll ask for help* in certain situations. Not many companies are looking for 22-year-old know-it-alls.
- Admit that *you don't have all the answers.* Or begin a lot of your answers with "I think..." or "From what I know about the industry..."
- *Don't sound squeamish* about going through the school of hard knocks. Many baby boomers think that baby busters—you and your friends—have severe "attitude problems." Tell the interviewer, "Sure, I know this position has its share of unpleasant duties, but I'm sure everyone that's had this job has learned a lot by doing them."
- Don't be afraid to admit that *you didn't have all of the answers* when you were 18 or 19. How many people know from the start that they wanted to be accountants or hospital administrators? Most interviewers will not be surprised by changes of major or evidence of indecision in your underclassmen days. Admit that it took you a while to find the direction you wanted to go in, but show how your other studies make you a great candidate.

Chapter 12

Wrapping it Up

Okay, you've made it this far, so there's absolutely no way to screw it up, right? Let's face it, you must have the job by now, or why would this incredibly energetic interviewer have asked you the 94 questions in the preceding chapters?

The end of an interview is a long good-bye. Inexperienced interviewers will usually run through a mental checklist to make sure they've asked you everything they should have.

We'll discuss the toughest of these wrap-up questions first, and then coast our way to the end with some questions that are easier, but which you should think about before sitting in front of the Grand Inquisitor.

Don't be a Know-It-All

Here is a seemingly innocuous question that, like "Tell me about yourself," has torpedoed many a job candidacy:

95. Do you have any questions?

When asked why a certain candidate is unsuccessful, many a hiring manager will say, "Oh, she was unprepared.

She didn't even ask me any questions." Never, *never*, I repeat, **never** say "no" the first time an interviewer asks if you have any questions.

How can you make one of the most important decisions of your life—whether or not to work for a particular company at a particular job and with a particular boss—with*out* asking questions?

What is an interviewer supposed to think about a prospective employee who would make a decision as important as that one without looking for more information?

What Do You Want to Know?

Keep in mind that the interview is a two-way street. The interviewer is trying to gain confidence in your ability and commitment. At the same time, *you* should be trying to determine whether or not this situation is right for you, whether it is worthy of your talents and commitment.

Here is a list of generic questions that you can ask when the interviewer gives you the opportunity to find out more about the company, the job, and the hiring manager:

- Can you give me a written description of the position, the major activities it involves, and the results expected?

If one does not exist, ask the interviewer to dictate as complete a description of the job to you as possible. It's an especially good idea to ask the *screening interviewer* for the job description—it'll help prepare you for your interview with the hiring manager.

- Does this job usually lead to other positions at the company? Which ones?

Do you want to work at a dead-end job? Of course not. Find out where you can expect the position you're interviewing for to take you. Ask the interviewer what has happened to the person you would be replacing. Where did he or she go in the company?

Of course, while pursuing this line of questioning, you don't want to make it seem as if you can't wait to get out of a job you don't even have yet! Ask these questions in a completely non-threatening manner, expressing a modicum, *not* an overabundance, of ambition.

- Can you tell me some of the particular skills or attributes that you want in the candidate for this position?

Not only will the answer tell you how much the interviewer will value some of your traits, but it will help you know how to respond during the remainder of the interview.

- Can you tell me a little bit about the people with whom I'll be working most closely?

I wish people had told me about this question before my last job interview! The answer can tell you many things: How good the people you are working with will be. How much you can learn from them. And, most importantly, whether the hiring manager is enthusiastic about his or her subordinates.

Remember, a hiring manager usually tries to put his best face on during an interview, just as the candidate does. He most likely will be in his most chipper mood (or, at least, pretending to be). Asking about the people he supervises every day can let you get a glimpse behind the "game face."

If asking about his subordinates elicits no obvious enthusiasm, you probably won't enjoy working for that hiring manager. He probably attributes little of his success, but most of his headaches, to the people who work for him.

- What do you like best about this company? Why?

This might seem like something you shouldn't ask under any circumstances, but it's too good a question *not* to ask.

If the boss hems and haws a lot over this one, it indicates that he doesn't like the company that much at all.

If he's enthusiastic, his answer should help sell you on him and the company.

The answer to this question can give you a good sense of the values of the organization *and* the hiring manager. If he talks about nothing but products and how well his stock options are doing, it indicates a lack of enthusiasm for the people side of the business and the company's philosophy.

Intelligent Questions for *You* to Ask About the Company

During your interview, the company should be selling you on the fact that it's a great place to work. Here are some questions to ask that will help fill in the blanks of your research into the organization:

- What is the company's ranking within the industry? Does this position represent a change from where it was a few years ago?

You should already have some indication of the answer to this question from your research, particularly if the company is publicly owned. If you have some of this information, build it into your question: "I've read that the company has risen from fifth to second in market share in just the past three years. What are the key reasons for this dramatic success?"

- What new products is the company considering introducing over the next year or two?

- Has the organization had any layoffs or reductions in its work force over the past couple of years: Are any others anticipated: Was *this* department affected. How much?

- Is the company considering entering any new markets during the next few years? Which ones?

- You say you are anticipating a growth rate of "x" percent over the next few years. Will this be accomplished internally or through acquisitions?

The interview is a great chance to learn a great deal about your prospective employer. Don't be too shy to ask the interview some of these questions.

However, you *should* be shy about asking about days off. *Never ask about vacation, holidays, sick pay, personal days, etc., with hiring managers.* It will make it seem as if you are looking for a chance to get out of the office *before you even start!*

You Want to be *Paid* for Working Here?

96. What sort of salary are you looking for?

The language most interviewers use to ask this question (they never say anything "indelicate" like: "How much money do you want in your paycheck?") indicates that no one likes to talk about money during interviews.

Of course, the unpleasantness of the topic doesn't mean you should avoid it completely. But in discussing salary, *timing is everything.*

My rule of thumb here is: You have absolutely *nothing* to gain by discussing dollars and cents *before* you've convinced the employer that you're the best person for the job.

Defer any question of salary that comes up early in the interview with an answer like this: "Colleen in Human Resources indicated the salary range for this position, and it seems about right to me."

This will give you a chance to prove how valuable you are before putting a price on your head. Wait until the offer stage to discuss your actual salary. That will help ensure that dollars and cents alone will not put you out of the running when the interviewer has been seeing other talent that might come cheap. At the offer stage, *you are the only candidate*—therefore, it is a good time to demand more.

I'm Worth It!

The usefulness of this strategy is brought home by the example of Harry, a friend of mine who not only was eminently qualified, he was also one heck of a good interview—and he knew it.

A recruiter called Harry one day and told him about a job that sounded perfect. But the recruiter, Gretchen, had one problem: The job was paying $40,000, and Harry needed more dough to pay the mortgage.

Harry told the interviewer firmly: "I want that job. Send me on the interview. After they've met me, they'll be willing to pay me what I want."

It sounded cocky, but Harry was absolutely right. He studiously avoided the subject of salary during the entire interview. However, at the offer stage, when the interviewer finally asked, "What would it take to get you over here?", Harry said, "I understand the job has a top salary of $40,000." He waited for the interviewer to nod, then said, "Well, I would need more than that. I came here because the job sounded terrific. In fact, the job description Gretchen gave me and which you just elaborated on has my name written all over it."

Eventually the employer came around to meet Harry's demand. But only because Harry had already *sold* himself. Asking for more money early in the interview most probably would have sunk Harry's chances to get the job at all.

Details, Details

---

97. Are you willing to travel?

Yes, of course you are. You have a terrific family that understands that business demands occasionally might call you away from home. Does that mean you want to be away three weeks out of four? Probably not. Unless you are unwilling to travel at all, don't let this question cost you the job. (If the job requires far more travel than you are prepared for, what are you doing on the interview?)

---

98. Are you willing to relocate?

If you really are: "Absolutely. In fact, I would look forward to the chance to live elsewhere and experience different types of people, learn a new geography."

*If you are **not:*** "Well, not unless the job is so terrific that it would be worth the upheaval of uprooting my family and leaving my relatives and friends. Does this position require a move? I'm obviously very interested in it, so I might consider relocating."

99. May I contact your current employer?

Why do people ask this question? You probably will feel like saying, "Sure, after you give me this job and I don't have to worry about getting canned because I've been out looking for another job."

Instead, you'll make yourself look much better by saying: "Sure you can, after we come to an agreement. I think it's best if they hear about this from me first."

100. May I contact your references?

Of course she can. Tell the interviewer that you will get back to her with a list of references that afternoon or, if it already is afternoon, the very next day.

Will this stalling make you seem unprepared? Shouldn't you go into the interview with the list already prepared? After all, your resume says (or should say) "References available upon request." Well, here's the request.

Frankly, in the world of interviews, stalling for a little time before giving references is SOP (standard operating procedure). The reason you want to wait is so you can tell your prospective references that a call might be coming from Mr. Krueger of Trikadekaphophia, Inc. If your references are indeed going to say wonderful things about you, they should be prepared to do so.

Over and Out

Okay, so you've answered all 100 questions put to y~~ ~~ far, and you're feeling as though you've just gone 14 rou~~nds~~ with Mike Tyson. What more could there be? Well, just one more little jab before the final bell:

101. Is there anything else about you I should know?

You might not think you have anything else left to say, but you'd better have! Here's someone giving you a chance to *close the sale* and you're just going to walk out of the room?

Of course you're not!

And sure, you might *not* have anything else to say, but, by God, you'll never admit it.

Develop a short answer to this question, one that plays upon your strengths, accomplishments, skills, and areas of knowledge. For instance: "Mr. Krueger, I think we've covered everything, but I want to reemphasize the key strengths that I would bring to this position.

"Experience: The job I'm currently in is quite similar to this one, and I would be excited by the chance to apply what I've learned at WidgetLand to your company.

"Management skill: I run a department almost equal in size to this one, and I'm a fair, effective supervisor.

"A record of success: I've won two prestigious industry awards. I would bring that creativity here.

"I am very excited about the prospect of working with you here at Trikadekaphobia. When do you expect to make a decision?"

This type of answer should summarize the points that *you* wanted to make during the interview. Notice that the last sentence asks Mr. Krueger to take some action, an effective selling technique that should give you a good indication of your chances of getting the job.

Did We Cover All of the Bases?

No.

We have dealt with the 101 questions that you'll most likely face during interviews. However, some interviewers will come up with humdingers that even I couldn't imagine. How will you handle them? If you have developed your personal inventory, practiced answers to the most common questions you should expect to be asked, developed a list of questions to ask the interviewer and done all your homework about the company—you'll answer them very well indeed, even if they are a bit of a shock at first.

Then there are the questions that interviewers might pose to you that are flat-out illegal and, in most cases, shouldn't be answered at all—"Oh, you just got married? Do you plan to have children soon?" "Rutigliano, huh? What part of Italy are your people from?" "Why isn't a pretty girl like you married, or are you engaged?" "How old are you?"

For more information on these questions, I have a bonus for you—chapter 13, "Your Rights as an Interviewee." It discusses in detail the kinds of questions you *shouldn't* expect to be asked on *any* interview—and what to do if you are.

I'm sure that the work this book asks you to put in will result in a terrific interview and a wonderful job. Take some small comfort in the fact that if I'm right, your work has only just begun.

Wrapping Up a Successful Interview

- *Be prepared* with a list of questions to ask the interviewer.
- Remember that *the interview is a two-way street*. Your job during it is to find out if the company, the industry, and the hiring manager are right for *you*. Don't be shy about asking the interviewer some rather tough questions.
- *Don't ask about days off* during the interview.
- *Don't ask about salary or benefits* until the offer stage. You do not want money to be a factor when the interviewer is considering whether or not you are the best person for the job.
- *Prepare a closing argument* that will briefly summarize your strengths, skills and accomplishments.
- *Don't give the names of your references* without telling them they might be hearing from your prospective new employer. And tell them anything you want particularly stressed (or left out).

Chapter 13

Your Rights as an Interviewee

In an ideal world, companies and managers would judge their employees only on the basis of their job performance, and candidates would be judged only against a set of criteria deemed important for doing the job right.

Our world isn't ideal. And in the *real* world, many managers and entire companies discriminate, and few people can judge others with pure objectivity.

The most unpleasant manifestations of the real world for too many job candidates are questions and remarks related to sex, race, ethnic background, marital status, and all of the other ridiculous traits upon which the ignorant and sometimes not so ignorant think it fair to judge people.

What can you do if you come face to face with racism, sexism, or some other ugly "ism" during a job interview?

All too many candidates feel that they have to endure and answer politely every question an interviewer asks, no matter how distasteful or irrelevant.

That's pure nonsense. Candidates have rights. And the interviewer should know what these rights are. At the very least, *you* should know what your rights are.

This chapter will explain your rights as an interviewee and what you can do if you feel an interviewer has acted inappropriately or unlawfully.

What Does *That* Have to Do With My Job?

It's pretty easy to tell when a question is inappropriate—it has little or nothing to do with how the candidate might perform on the job. And that's pretty much what the law states—interviewers can ask questions that have to do with *job performance*. When they ask questions that are unrelated to the work to be performed, they could be walking on thin ice.

Every state has fair-employment-practices laws governing the screening of job candidates and lists of questions considered unlawful for employers to ask on job applications and during interviews. Check with your state's Fair Employment Practices Commission for more details.

In the meantime, I can give you the following general guidelines that may help you recognize discriminatory or otherwise illegal interview and job application questions:

- *Name*. Sure, that seems innocent enough. Employers will need your name to give you a paycheck, if for no other reason. But in many states, you are protected from questions that seek to determine your birth name if you've had it legally changed, or, if you are a married woman, your maiden name. However, employers *are* permitted to ask what other names they should check to determine your employment history.

- *Creed*. Under no circumstances is an employer permitted to ask about your religious affiliation or the religious holidays you observe. In addition, interviewers are not permitted to make even simple statements such as, "This is a Christian (or Jewish, or Muslim) company." Perhaps they are looking for some sort of reaction from the prospective employee, and plan to make a hiring decision based on that "pro" or "con" reaction.

- *Nationality*. Employers are generally forbidden to ask about your ancestry, descent, parentage, or nationality, that of your parents or spouse, or inquire about your "mother tongue." Technically speaking, an interviewer could not ask, "Is that an Irish name?" but he *could* ask you what language(s) you are proficient in. A tricky way, he or she may hope, to get the same answer.

- *Race*. Employers cannot ask you about the color of your skin or that of your relatives or spouse.

- *Sex*. Employers are not permitted to ask about a candidate's marital status or plans for marriage. Likewise, they are forbidden from asking women about their plans for having children.

  I think this is an area where it is very easy for *you* to "open the door" to a host of questions you aren't required to answer—*unless you bring them up*. After all, what could seem more innocent than chit-chatting about your fiance or spouse or kids? And you *really* want to discuss your tentative plan for having a child within a year, right?

- *Military service*. The employer can ask how long and in what branch of the service you were in, but not the type of discharge you received.

- *Age*. Employers cannot ask for your birth date or about facts that might reveal your birth date, such as the year you graduated from high school. (Though a glance through a resume should readily provide this information.)

- *Physical condition.* Employers can ask if you have any physical conditions that might *impede your performance on the job,* but they cannot ask something like, "Do you have any physical disabilities?"

- *Photograph.* Employers are not allowed to ask you to affix a photograph to your job application.

- *Organizations.* Employers can ask about the applicant's membership in organizations that *the applicant* considers important to the performance of the job. Otherwise, this can be another sneaky way to find out about religion (you're a member of B'nai B'rith or the Christian Church Fellowship), race (you're a member of the NAACP and it's not obvious you are Afro-American), political affiliation, etc.

How to React When Asked the Wrong Question

Despite a plethora of lawsuits charging employers with discriminatory hiring practices over the past 25 years, unlawful questions still are commonly asked during interviews. This is particularly true of interviews by hiring managers, who generally have not received the extensive education on legal issues personnel professionals routinely undergo.

What do you do if you're asked an unlawful question you believe you shouldn't have to answer? You have three choices:

1. You can be a Constitutionalist and refuse on principle to answer any unlawful question, even if you'd come up smelling like a rose.

2. You can be a pragmatist and provide any answers you feel wouldn't hurt you, while you tactfully side-step illegal questions you think *could* hurt you.

3. You can use a mixture of both approaches.

Let's say you have an "obviously" Italian last name, like Rutigliano. You greet the interviewer and he says, "Boy, that's Italian, isn't it?" You should smile politely and not answer at all. It is quite possible he meant absolutely no offense.

However, if later the interviewer pursues the line of questioning with, "Were your parents born in the United States or on the other side?", you can dodge it one more time by saying something like, "They don't remember. They were just little babies." But by now you should be wary for any further signs of prejudice or insensitivity.

If the interviewer still doesn't get the hint and continues to allude to your Italian heritage, then you should point out to him that he is doing something illegal. You might say, "I really don't see what my ancestry has to do with my application for this job. You must know that you're not supposed to ask me questions like this."

Believe it or not, you could still stay on the interviewer's good side if you handle the situation in a diplomatic way. At the same time, you will have put him on notice that you are aware of the law and do not take it as lightly as he obviously does. You also have told him that he has opened himself up to a discrimination charge.

Such a line of questioning, however, might well indicate that you don't want to work for this supervisor under any circumstances. He's obviously an ignorant, insensitive person.

If you don't *care* that he's an insensitive boob—you just want the job, and he can talk about your name, creed, religion or marriage plans all day—then bring a thick skin to the interview and don't make an issue out of his comments.

They Are Usually Much More Subtle

However, many employers or supervisors that discriminate will try to elicit information they consider damaging in more subtle ways.

For instance, an interviewer might ask older applicants what year they graduated college. Or ask someone he suspects of being an immigrant if English is spoken at home.

Here's a case of a *really* subtle form of discrimination. A friend of mine applied for a job at one of the big tobacco concerns. She went through three interviews, and the company was obviously very high on her. During her last interview, she was asked if she would like a cigarette. She said, "No thanks. I don't smoke," and that was the last she heard from them.

Notice, the interviewer never asked, "Are you a smoker?" or "Do you smoke?" Turning down an applicant because she refused to engage in an unhealthy activity might put the company on questionable legal and public relations ground.

But the information was gotten nevertheless, and the hiring decision was made based on that illicit information.

(When I heard the story, I couldn't help but wish she had answered, "No thanks. I don't smoke *during interviews."* Perfectly true, and nearly as coy as their gambit!)

Still another female acquaintance, Karen, interviewed at one of the largest companies in the U.S. The skilled interviewer kept shifting gears between very job-related and very personal questions. Though Karen was a savvy interviewee and had little trouble deflecting the questions she knew to be inappropriate, she let her guard down once, beginning an answer with "My husband..."

The interviewer pounced as quickly as a salesman's foot in an open door. She began asking questions about what the husband did and how he "felt about his wife having a job."

The interviewer apparently wanted to know what Karen's career and family plans were, but knew better than to come right out and ask such unlawful questions.

Once *Karen* introduced the subject of her husband, however, the interviewer felt her "family life" was fair game. After all, she didn't want to ask anything as obviously unlawful as, "Are you married?" or "Don't you want to have children, and won't your career interfere with that." She just wanted to know the *answers* to those questions.

Therefore, I'd advise you never to bring up personal material that you might not want to talk about in more detail. Savvy interviewers will grab at the opportunity to get information they want without running the risk of ending up in court. Their defense will be, "*I* never asked about her family; *she* brought it up."

And while it still might not be entirely "up and up," it may well prove enough of a defense.

What To Do After the Fact

If you are not offered a position after being asked unlawful questions, you *might* have grounds for charging the employer with discrimination. The interviewer asked non-job-related questions, and you believe your refusal to answer these questions or the answers you provided led to your not being hired.

The operative word here is "might." You would have to prove that the questions were asked for the purpose of discriminating among applicants for an illegal reason.

For instance, if the manager asking all those questions about Italian ancestry subsequently hired another Italian, you wouldn't have much of a claim, despite the fact that you *were* asked illegal questions.

If you *do* think that you have grounds for a charge of discrimination, you should file your charges simultaneously with the appropriate state agency and the federal government's Equal Employment Opportunity Commission (EEOC). The EEOC generally will wait until the state agency has conducted an investigation, then conduct an investigation of its own.

As you would expect when dealing with government agencies, you might not hear anything for years, and when they do act, it is solely to determine whether there is reason to believe your charge is true. Therefore, if you are anxious for justice, you should request that the EEOC issue you a notice to sue 180 days after you file your charge.

If You Are Right

If the EEOC determines in you favor, it will attempt to mediate the dispute between you and the employer. Failing to arrange for such an agreement, the Commission will either file a suit or issue you a letter giving you the right to sue the employer. You must file your suit within 90 days of receiving such a letter.

Even if you go through all this trouble and win your lawsuit, don't expect to receive one of those colossal jury awards that seem to occur weekly on "L.A. Law." The most you'll probably get from the employer is about one year's salary.

Handling Illegal Questions

- *Know your rights.* And what questions are out of bounds.

- *Don't bring up subjects* you really don't want to talk about or that get into areas you don't feel are any of the interviewer's business. Doing so might allow the interview to ask what *would* have been illegal questions...*if you hadn't opened the door first.*

- If you feel that the interviewer is asking you questions that shouldn't be asked, the first step is to try to *shrug them off and change the direction* of the conversation.

- If that doesn't work, *inform the employer that you know he or she is doing something unlawful.* This will give him or her a subtle warning that you won't submit to illegal interview behavior, or the discrimination that might result from it, without a fight.

- If it still doesn't work, *terminate the interview* and, possibly, seek to bring formal charges against the company and the interviewer.

- But remember, you are there because you wanted a job. And you always have to weigh how strongly you want to react to such questions against your need for that job.

    Many hiring managers will not even know they are doing something wrong, so giving them the benefit of the doubt (though not an answer) may be in order. It's *your* call.

- But would you *really* want to work at a company or for a person that couldn't take the series of hints you've given?

Important note: None of the advice in this chapter should be construed as constituting legal advice. I am not an attorney. If you feel a would-be employer has discriminated against you, you should contact the appropriate government agencies and a competent attorney to assess your rights and options under state and federal law.

Chapter 14

The 101 Toughest Interview Questions

Chapter 5

Chapter 6

Chapter 7

Chapter 8

Chapter 9

Chapter 10

Chapter 11

Chapter 12

Index

Don't Miss These Other Ron Fry Best Sellers

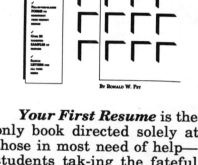

Your First Interview tells you how to conduct yourself during every phase of the interview process. What to wear, how to prepare, how to handle illegal questions, how to field the offer, make the most of salary negotiations, close the deal.

In short, it shows how to take control of the process— to sell the company on you, and to make sure *you're* sold on the company.

Your First Interview, ISBN 0-934829-67.5, Paper, 160 pp., $8.95

Your First Resume is the only book directed solely at those in most need of help— students tak-ing the fateful "next step," returning servicemen and -women, and anyone reentering the workforce after a long absence.

Includes numerous examples and fill-in forms for resumes, evaluations, letters and more.

Your First Resume, 2nd Edition, ISBN 0-934829-55-1, 192 pp., Paper, $10.95

To Order Either Or Both Books, Call Toll-Free
1-800-CAREER-1 Today

Or send a check or money order for the full purchase price plus $2.50 per order (shipping) and $1.00 per book (handling) to: The Career Press, PO Box 34, Hawthorne, NJ 07507